Gary Sherman

The PyQGIS Programmer's Guide

Extending QGIS 2.x with Python

loca🎯e
PRESS

Credits & Copyright

THE PYQGIS PROGRAMMER'S GUIDE
EXTENDING QGIS 2.X WITH PYTHON

by Gary Sherman

Published by Locate Press LLC

Direct permission requests to gsherman@locatepress.com or mail:
Locate Press LLC, PO Box 671897, Chugiak, AK, USA, 99567-1897

Cover Design Julie Springer
Interior Design Based on Tufte-LATEXdocument class
Publisher Website http://locatepress.com
Book Website http://locatepress.com/ppg

Contents

List of Figures

Listings

1

Introduction

Welcome to the world of PyQGIS, the blending of Python and Quantum GIS[1] to extend and enhance your open source GIS toolbox. With PyQGIS you can write scripts and plugins to implement new features and perform automated tasks.

This book will guide you in getting started with PyQGIS. After a brief introduction to Python, you'll learn how to understand the QGIS Application Programmer Interface (API), write scripts, and build a plugin.

This book is designed to allow you to work through the examples as we go along. At the end of most chapters you will find a set of exercises you can do to enhance your learning experience.

1.1 Requirements

To learn PyQGIS you need several pieces of software:

- A working QGIS 2.0 install on Linux, Mac, or Windows
- Python 2.x
- Qt[2]
- PyQt[3]

Before you dive in and start installing the components needed to work with PyQGIS, take a look at Chapter 3, Setting Up Your Development Tools, on page 35. You may already have everything you need to get started.

[1] At version 2.0, the "Quantum" was dropped from the name and the project is now simply referred to as QGIS.

You must use Python 2.x; QGIS does not support Python 3.x.

[2] http://loc8.cc/ppg/qt
[3] http://qt-project.org

1.2 Sample Data

In order to work through the examples in the book you'll need some data. For vector data, it will be best for you to use the sample data used throughout the book. You can download the sample vector data set at:

```
http://locatepress.com/ppg/data_code
```

Unzip it to a convenient location that you can remember.

For raster layers, download one of the Natural Earth rasters available at:

Note: The Natural Earth rasters can be quite large.

```
http://loc8.cc/ppg/natural_earth
```

We renamed the `.tif` from the download to `natural_earth.tif` and you'll see it referred to that way in the text.

If you are familiar with vector and raster data, feel free to use your own and adapt the commands/examples accordingly.

1.3 Code

All of the code examples in this book are available for download at:

```
http://locatepress.com/ppg/data_code
```

You are encouraged to work through the examples on your own, but feel free to copy and paste.

1.4 Conventions Used in this Book

Generally speaking, URLs are shortened using the `loc8.cc` domain. The exception is where the URL points to a top-level domain or to a site that is unlikely to change. This allows us to keep the book up to date when sites move or reorganize their content.

This book contains code examples, interactive Python sessions, and notes/tips. The convention for each of these is illustrated below:

Code listings:

Code listings are presented in a fixed width font and may or may not include line numbers:

```
 1    """
 2    ScriptRunner is the main plugin class that initializes the QGIS
 3    plugin, initializes the GUI, and performs the work.
 4    """
 5
 6    def __init__(self, iface):
 7        """
 8        Save reference to the QGIS interface
 9        """
10        self.iface = iface
```

Python console sessions:

Input lines in an interactive session (something you typed) are prefaced with the >>> prompt. Indented lines in a block are preceded with ... and output from the interpreter is shown without any leading characters:

```
>>> my_list = ['north', 'south', 'east', 'west']
>>> my_list[1]
'south'
>>> for d in my_list:
...     print d
...
north
south
east
west
```

Notes/Tips:

 This icon is used to indicate a helpful note or tip.

Screenshots:

Screenshots throughout the book are a mix of those taken from Linux, Mac OS X, and Windows versions of QGIS 2.0.

1.5 Your First PyQGIS experiment

Let's get a taste of PyQGIS right up front. For this experiment, we'll use the Python console in QGIS to manipulate the view. First we need a layer to work with and we'll assume that you have downloaded the sample data.

Open QGIS and load the world_borders.shp file using the Add Vector Layer menu.

The first thing we need to do is open the Python console by choosing `Plugins->Python Console` from the menu. This gives us a window that looks a lot like a command or terminal window with a prompt.

For this experiment we'll be using methods (think functions) defined by the *QgisInterface* class:

- *zoomFull()*
- *zoomToPrevious()*
- *zoomToNext()*
- *showAttributeTable()*
- *showLayerProperties()*

The `iface` object gives you access to a wide range of QGIS objects and classes.

When you open the console, there is a hint on getting help on using the `iface` object. Using the built-in `help` function you can get a list of the methods and functions defined in the `QgisInterface` class:

```
help(iface)
Help on QgisInterface in module qgis.gui object:

class QgisInterface(PyQt4.QtCore.QObject)
 |  QgisInterface()
 |
 |  Method resolution order:
 |      QgisInterface
 |      PyQt4.QtCore.QObject
 |      sip.wrapper
 |      sip.simplewrapper
 |      __builtin__.object
 |
 |  Methods defined here:
 |
 |  composerAdded = <unbound signal composerAdded>
 |  composerWillBeRemoved = <unbound signal composerWillBeRemoved>
 |  currentLayerChanged = <unbound signal currentLayerChanged>
 |  initializationCompleted = <unbound signal initializationCompleted>
 |  newProjectCreated = <unbound signal newProjectCreated>
 |  projectRead = <unbound signal projectRead>
 |  ----------------------------------------------------------------
 |  Data and other attributes defined here:
 |
 |  actionAbout = <built-in function actionAbout>
 |  actionAddAllToOverview = <built-in function actionAddAllToOverview>
 |  actionAddFeature = <built-in function actionAddFeature>
 |  actionAddOgrLayer = <built-in function actionAddOgrLayer>
```

```
|
|  ...
|
|   zoomFull = <built-in function zoomFull>
|   zoomToActiveLayer = <built-in function zoomToActiveLayer>
|   zoomToNext = <built-in function zoomToNext>
|   zoomToPrevious = <built-in function zoomToPrevious>
```

We only listed the first few and last four functions supported by `iface`. Later we'll show you another way to get at this information using the QGIS online API documentation.

Manipulating the View

Let's use `iface` to manipulate the view. With the mouse, zoom into any area of the world you like. Now we will use the console to zoom back to the full extent:

```
iface.zoomFull()
```

When you press enter, the map is zoomed back out to the full extent of the `world_borders` layer.

Now try:

```
iface.zoomToPrevious()
```

This zooms us to the previous view, which happens to be the area you zoomed to with the mouse. If you try `iface.zoomToNext()`, you'll find it gives the same result as `iface.zoomFull()`.

Using the Active Layer

To illustrate a couple of other methods, we'll open the attribute table and the layer properties dialog for the active layer. First we have to get a reference to the active layer. Make sure the `world_borders` layer is highlighted in the layer list, then in the console enter:

```
active_layer = iface.activeLayer()
```

Once we have a reference to the active layer, we can use the following to open both its attribute table and the layer properties:

```
iface.showAttributeTable(active_layer)
iface.showLayerProperties(active_layer)
```

Here is what the complete console session looks like:

```
Python 2.7.2 (default, Oct 11 2012, 20:14:37)
## Type help(iface) for more info and list of methods.

>>> iface
<qgis.gui.QgisInterface object at 0x115d78170>
>>> iface.zoomFull()
>>> iface.zoomToPrevious()
>>> iface.zoomToNext()
>>> active_layer = iface.activeLayer()
>>> active_layer
<qgis.core.QgsVectorLayer object at 0x1116c4440>
>>> iface.showAttributeTable(active_layer)
>>> iface.showLayerProperties(active_layer)
```

If you look at the documentation for the *QgisInterface* class you'll see it has a lot more methods than those we just used. We'll talk more about the QGIS API in a later chapter. This tour of the console has given you a small taste of what you can accomplish using PyQGIS. We'll dive in further when we get to Chapter 6, Using the Console, on page 61.

Let's move on to a brief introduction to Python. If you're already a Python guru, or at least comfortable with the basics, feel free to move on to Chapter 3, Setting Up Your Development Tools, on page 35.

1.6   Exercises

To complete the exercises, you'll need to look at the QGIS API documentation found at `http://loc8.cc/ppg/iface`

1. Using the *QgisInterface* documentation, determine what method you would use to open one of your saved QGIS project files (`.qgs`) using the console.

2. Determine which method you would use to add a raster layer to the map.

3. Adding a shapefile to the map requires the full path to the layer, a short name (basename), and a provider key ('ogr'). Using the console, add the `world_borders` shapefile to the map.

2

Python Basics

This book is not a Python tutorial—we'll give you a short introduction to concepts needed to get started with PyQGIS. As you get into it, you'll likely want to dig a little deeper into Python to improve your skills.

We won't talk much about flow control, variables, operators, and all the other things you need to know to use the language. For that, see the list of additional resources at the end of the chapter.

2.1 *Getting Help*

We already saw an example of using the help function to produce a nicely formatted description of the *QgisInterface* class. This works both from the command line and in the QGIS Python Console. Another helpful function is dir, which provides a list of all the methods and functions for an object. Although terse, this can be helpful if you have forgotten the name of a function.

The help function can be used on individual methods to provide more detail. In exercises for the last chapter, we used the addVectorLayer method to add a shapefile to the map. If we examine the help for this method we get:

```
help(iface.addVectorLayer)
Help on built-in function addVectorLayer:
```

```
addVectorLayer(...)
    QgisInterface.addVectorLayer(QString, QString, QString)
        -> QgsVectorLayer
```

See QString in the *Python and C++ Types* table in Section 5.2 on page 49.

This not only shows us that the method requires three string arguments, but also tells us it returns a `QgsVectorLayer` object. While helpful, your best resource is the QGIS API online documentation, which we cover in Chapter 5, Navigating the QGIS API, on page 49.

2.2 Data Structures

When working with PyQGIS and the QGIS API, you'll typically need to know something about the following:

- Lists
- Tuples
- Dictionaries
- Classes

The list Type

A `list` is similar to an array of items, stored in sequential order:

```
>>> my_list = ["GIS", "QGIS", "Python", 1, "open source"]
>>> my_list[0]
'GIS'
>>> my_list[1:3]
['QGIS', 'Python']
>>>
>>> my_list[-1]
'open source'
```

Here you can see we created a `list` containing five items, four strings and one integer. A `list` uses a zero-based index to refer to an item. As you can see from the above example, you can use the colon notation to refer to a range of items in the `list`. To get the last item in a `list`, use [-1].

You can mix object types in a `list`, including adding other lists:

```
>>> new_list = ["apple", my_list]
>>> new_list
['apple', ['GIS', 'QGIS', 'Python', 1, 'open source']]
>>> new_list[1]
['GIS', 'QGIS', 'Python', 1, 'open source']
>>> new_list[1][2]
```

```
'Python'
```

A `list` is iterable, meaning you can traverse each item:

```
>>> for item in my_list:
...       print item
...
GIS
QGIS
Python
1
open source
```

There are a number of other operations you can do on a `list`, including append, pop, remove, sort, and reverse.

The tuple

A tuple is simply an immutable `list`, meaning once created, you can't change it in any way. You access the items in a tuple the same way you do in a `list`:

```
>>> my_tuple = ("GIS", "QGIS", "Python", 1, "open source")
>>> my_tuple
('GIS', 'QGIS', 'Python', 1, 'open source')
>>> my_tuple[0]
'GIS'
>>> my_tuple[-1]
'open source'
```

While we can change the value of an item in a list, you can't do that with a tuple:

```
>>> my_list
['GIS', 'QGIS', 'Python', 1, 'open source']
>>> my_list[1] = 'QGIS 2.0'
>>> my_list
['GIS', 'QGIS 2.0', 'Python', 1, 'open source']
>>> my_tuple
('GIS', 'QGIS', 'Python', 1, 'open source')
>>> my_tuple[1] = 'QGIS 2.0'
Traceback (most recent call last):
  File "<stdin>", line 1, in <module>
TypeError: 'tuple' object does not support item assignment
```

Tuples are faster than lists; use them when you need to iterate over a data structure that never needs to change.

Using Tuples - Examples where you might want to use a tuple include days of the week or months of the year. These never change and you can iterate over them quicker with a tuple.

Lastly, you can convert between tuples and lists:

```
>>> a_tuple = tuple(my_list)
>>> a_tuple
('GIS', 'QGIS 2.0', 'Python', 1, 'open source')
>>> a_list = list(my_tuple)
>>> a_list
['GIS', 'QGIS', 'Python', 1, 'open source']
```

The dict

In Python, a `dict` implements a dictionary object, also known as a hash, hash table, or map in other languages. It consists of a set of keys and related values, providing the ability to do an indexed lookup:

```
>>> my_dictionary = {"qgis":"c++", "grass":"c", "udig":"java"}
>>> my_dictionary['udig']
'java'
>>> my_dictionary['qgis']
'c++'
>>> my_dictionary['grass']
'c'
```

Here we created a dictionary that "maps" an open source application to its underlying language. We can reference the language a particular application is written in using the name as the key.

We can also create a dictionary using:

```
>>> my_dictionary = dict(qgis='c++', grass='c', udig='java')
>>> my_dictionary
{'qgis': 'c++', 'udig': 'java', 'grass': 'c'}
```

A dictionary can be modified by assigning values to new or existing keys:

```
>>> my_dictionary['mapnik'] = "c++"
>>> my_dictionary['qgis'] ="c++/python"
>>> my_dictionary
{'qgis': 'c++/python', 'grass': 'c', 'mapnik': 'c++', 'udig': 'java'}
```

We can get both the keys and values of a `dict` as a list:

```
>>> list(my_dictionary)
['qgis', 'grass', 'mapnik', 'udig']
>>> my_dictionary.keys()
['qgis', 'grass', 'mapnik', 'udig']
>>> my_dictionary.values()
['c++/python', 'c', 'c++', 'java']
```

By default, the list function converts the keys of a `dict` to a `list`.

We can check to see if a `dict` contains a certain key value:

```
>>> 'qgis' in my_dictionary
True
>>> 'postgis' in my_dictionary
False
```

This is important; if you try to access a non-existent key you'll be greeted with an error:

```
>>> my_dictionary['qgis']
'c++/python'
>>> my_dictionary['postgis']
Traceback (most recent call last):
  File "<stdin>", line 1, in <module>
KeyError: 'postgis'
```

Before you access a value, you can check to see if it exists to prevent an error:

Previously you would use the has_key function to check the existence of a value in a dictionary. That method is now deprecated and the use of "in" is preferred.

```
>>> my_dictionary = {"qgis":"c++", "grass":"c", "udig":"java"}
>>> if 'qgis' in my_dictionary:
...     print my_dictionary['qgis']
... else:
...     print "The key 'qgis' does not exist"

c++/python
```

The alternative (and often preferred) method is to wrap the code in a try/except block:

```
>>> try:
...     print my_dictionary['postgis']
... except:
...     print "Key not found"
...
Key not found
```

2.3 Classes

Classes are an integral part of Python and you'll be working with them extensively when programming PyQGIS. Python classes, just like their counterparts in other object oriented languages, can have methods and attributes, allowing you to model objects. In QGIS there are a large number of classes representing map layers, data stores, legends, symbology, and much more.

If you look back to the first chapter, you'll recognize that we already worked with some QGIS classes when exploring the Python console.

When creating a class, you need to think in terms of attributes that describe it and what it can "do". Here is a simple Python class that begins to model a point:

Listing 2.1: simplepoint.py

```
1  class Point:
2
3      marker_size = 4
4
5      def draw(self):
6          print "drawing the point"
7
8      def move(self, new_x, new_y):
9          print "moving the point"
```

The Point class has one attribute, marker_size and two methods: draw and move. We can create and use the class as follows:

```
>>> from simplepoint import Point
>>> my_point = Point()
>>> my_point.marker_size
4
>>> my_point.draw()
drawing the point
>>> my_point.move()
moving the point
```

This trivial example of a class illustrates the basic concepts. Once you instantiate your class, you can access the attributes and call methods.

We'll use classes both in writing scripts that run from the console and in plugins.

Subclassing a Class

Frequently you may need to create a class that inherits behavior from an existing class. You do this by *subclassing* the class, which results in our new class inheriting all the features of its parent.

Take for example the *QgsPoint* class. Using dir(QgsPoint) we can get a list of its attributes:

```
>>> from qgis.core import QgsPoint
>>> dir(QgsPoint)
['__class__', '__delattr__', '__dict__', '__doc__',
```

```
'__eq__', '__format__', '__ge__', '__getattribute__',
'__getitem__', '__gt__', '__hash__', '__init__', '__le__',
'__len__', '__lt__', '__module__', '__ne__', '__new__',
'__reduce__', '__reduce_ex__', '__repr__', '__setattr__',
'__sizeof__', '__str__', '__subclasshook__',
'__weakref__', 'azimuth', 'multiply', 'onSegment', 'set',
'setX', 'setY', 'sqrDist', 'sqrDistToSegment',
'toDegreesMinutes', 'toDegreesMinutesSeconds', 'toString',
'wellKnownText', 'x', 'y']
```

Let's create a new class that adds a Z value to the QgsPoint class by sub-classing it:

Listing 2.2: point3d_1.py

```
1  from qgis.core import QgsPoint
2
3
4  class Point3D(QgsPoint):
5
6      def __init__(self, x, y, z):
7          super(Point3D, self).__init__(x, y)
8          self.z_value = z
9
10     def setZ(self, z):
11         self.z_value = z
12
13     def z(self):
14         return self.z_value
```

First we have to make sure we have imported the *QgsPoint* class from the qgis.core module. Then in *line 4* we define our new class *Point3D*, inheriting from *QgsPoint*. This will give our new class all the methods and attributes of *QgsPoint*, plus those we will add.

In *line 7* we call the base class *__init__* method, passing it the values of *x* and *y*. In *line 8* we set *z_value* using the *z* argument that was passed.

If you look back at the attributes of *QgsPoint*, you'll see there are methods to set the X and Y values, as well as return them. We need the same methods for our Z value. *Lines 10 and 11* set the Z value and in *lines 13 and 14* we provide the code needed to return it. Here is an example of how we can use our new class:

```
>>> from point3d import Point3D
>>> pt = Point3D(100, 100, 299)
```

```
>>> pt.z()
299
>>> pt.setZ(199)
>>> pt.z()
199
```

You can see our added methods work as expected. If we list the attributes of *Point3D*, you'll see all those of *QgsPoint*, as well as our new methods:

```
>>> dir(Point3D)
['__class__', '__delattr__', '__dict__', '__doc__',
'__eq__', '__format__', '__ge__', '__getattribute__',
'__getitem__', '__gt__', '__hash__', '__init__', '__le__',
'__len__', '__lt__', '__module__', '__ne__', '__new__',
'__reduce__', '__reduce_ex__', '__repr__', '__setattr__',
'__sizeof__', '__str__', '__subclasshook__',
'__weakref__', 'azimuth', 'multiply', 'onSegment', 'set',
'setX', 'setY', 'setZ', 'sqrDist', 'sqrDistToSegment',
'toDegreesMinutes', 'toDegreesMinutesSeconds', 'toString',
'wellKnownText', 'x', 'y', 'z']
```

There is a more work to do if we want to add full "Z" support to our new point class, such as overriding the *toString* and *wellKnownText* methods to include Z values. For example, if we call the *toString* method on our new class, it returns the X and Y values, but our Z value is nowhere to be found:

```
>>> pt.toString()
u'100, 100'
```

Let's override *toString* to include the Z value:

Listing 2.3: point3d.py

```
1   from qgis.core import QgsPoint
2
3
4   class Point3D(QgsPoint):
5
6       def __init__(self, x, y, z):
7           super(Point3D, self).__init__(x, y)
8           self.z_value = z
9
10      def setZ(self, z):
11          self.z_value = z
12
13      def z(self):
14          return self.z_value
15
16      def toString(self):
```

17   **return** u"{:.2f}, {:.2f}, {:.2f}".format(self.x(), self.y(), self.z())

Lines 16 and 17 implement the overridden *toString* method, returning a string with X, Y, Z values.[4]

[4] Since the original *toString* method returns a unicode string, we prefaced our return value with u to do the same.

```
>>> from point3d import Point3D
>>> pt = Point3D(100, 100, 199)
>>> pt.toString()
u'100.00, 100.00, 199.00'
```

We have a partially functioning 3D point object---you can complete it if you like.

Subclassing an existing object allows us to extend the capabilities of PyQGIS by taking advantage of all the power present in the API.

Where would we bother to subclass an object in PyQGIS? A common example is when creating a new map tool that operates on the map canvas. We can easily create our own map tool that emits the coordinates of a click on the map canvas by inheriting from *QgsMapToolEmitPoint*. This gives us access to the *canvasClicked* method (a signal) that provides us with both the location of the click and the mouse button that triggered it:

We talk more about signals and slots in Section 5.3, Signals and Slots, on page 51.

```
canvasClicked (const QgsPoint &point, Qt::MouseButton button)
```

The deeper you go into PyQGIS programming, the more you'll find cases where subclassing the QGIS API objects provides the functionality you need.

There's more to Python classes such as private variables and private methods. If you want to dig into the details, refer to some of the resources at the end of this chapter.

2.4 Strings, Ranges, and Other Handy Things

Let's take a quick look at some other handy things in Python that you will find useful.

Strings

You'll use strings everywhere in your code. In this section we'll use an interactive Python session to illustrate some of the concepts.

```
>>> s = "QGIS loves Python"
>>> # split on whitespace
... s.split()
['QGIS', 'loves', 'Python']
>>> # split into variables
... (a, b, c) = s.split()
>>> print a, b, c
QGIS loves Python
>>> # slice
... s[0:1]
'Q'
>>> s[-1:]
'n'
>>> s[:-1]
'QGIS loves Pytho'
>>> # split on a character
... s.split('o')
['QGIS l', 'ves Pyth', 'n']
```

Notice that in many of the string operations above, the result is a Python list.

Here are some additional things we can do with strings:

```
>>> s = 'qgis loves python'
>>> # title case
... s.title()
'Qgis Loves Python'
>>> # upper case
... s = 'qgis loves python'
>>> s = s.upper()
>>> s
'QGIS LOVES PYTHON'
>>> s.lower()
'qgis loves python'
```

We can find a substring using *in*:

```
>>> s = 'QGIS loves Python'
>>> # does substring exist?
... 'GIS' in s
True
>>> # where is it?
... s.find('GIS')
1
>>> s[1:]
'GIS loves Python'
```

Python comes with powerful string formatting capabilities. You can use either the *%* operator or the `format` method:

```
>>> s = 'loves'
>>> "QGIS %s Python" % s
'QGIS loves Python'
>>> "QGIS {} Python".format(s)
'QGIS loves Python'
>>> # with two strings:
... s2 = 'Python'
>>> "QGIS %s %s" % (s, s2)
'QGIS loves Python'
>>> "QGIS {} {}".format(s, s2)
'QGIS loves Python'
```

Which should you use? It depends on whether you need the full power of *format* or just need some simple formatting. The *format* method has a lot of options for formatting strings and numbers, as well as using named replacement fields:

```
>>> 'Location = {longitude}, {latitude}'.format(longitude=-150,
...                                       latitude=60.5)
'Location = -150, 60.5'
```

Using named replacements comes in handy when you need to format a string with a lot of parameters. For complete information on format specifiers, as well as other string operations, see the Python `string` documentation.[5]

[5] http://loc8.cc/ppg/py_string

Ranges

Ranges are handy when you need a list of integers to use in a *for* loop:

```
>>> range(0, 10)
[0, 1, 2, 3, 4, 5, 6, 7, 8, 9]
>>> range(1, 10, 2)
[1, 3, 5, 7, 9]
>>> range(100, 0, -10)
[100, 90, 80, 70, 60, 50, 40, 30, 20, 10]
```

The third argument in the `range` function specifies the step—by default 1.

Function and Method Arguments

In addition to "regular" arguments, Python allows you to use default and keyword arguments in your functions and methods.

In a function with default arguments you specify a value for each optional argument. Let's say we have a function that draws a circle:

```
def draw_circle(radius, color='blue', line_width=1):
    print radius, color, line_width
```

We can call this function in the following ways:

```
>>> draw_circle(10)
10 blue 1
>>> draw_circle(10, 'red')
10 red 1
>>> draw_circle(10, 'red', 2)
10 red 2
```

If we don't provide an argument, the default is used. Note we can't specify a line_width without first specifying the color—the arguments are positional.

Using keyword arguments, we can call the same function like this:

```
>>> draw_circle(10, color='red')
10 red 1
>>> draw_circle(10, line_width=2)
10 blue 2
>>> draw_circle(10, line_width=2, color='red')
10 red 2
>>> draw_circle(line_width=2, color='red', radius=15)
15 red 2
```

By using the *keyword=value* syntax, we can specify the arguments in any order. Those that we don't specify will use the default, assuming they are optional arguments. If we don't supply the mandatory radius argument, this happens:

```
>>> draw_circle(line_width=2, color='red')
Traceback (most recent call last):
  File "<stdin>", line 1, in <module>
TypeError: draw_circle() takes at least 1 argument (2 given)
```

The error seems misleading—the function takes at least one argument and we gave it two, yet it still complained. This is because *radius* is mandatory and we didn't supply it.

Another useful way to call our function is using a dictionary with the ** operator:

```
>>> args = {'color' : 'red', 'line_width' : 1.5, 'radius' : 20}
>>> draw_circle(**args)
20 red 1.5
>>> args = {'color' : 'red', 'radius' : 20}
>>> draw_circle(**args)
20 red 1
```

Here we passed the `args` dictionary to the function and it works similar to using named arguments. Notice in the last example, we didn't add the `line_width` to our dictionary and the function used the default value we specified in the function definition.

We've only touched on a small part of Python, but you'll see some of the things in the previous examples when we get into writing code. As always, refer to the documentation at `http://docs.python.org/2`.

2.5 Installing Packages

Eventually in your Python career you are going to want to install a package to provide some bit of functionality you need. There are literally thousands of packages available to extend Python's capability.

The "old" way to install packages was to use `easy_install`—this method still works today. The "new" way is to use `pip`.[6]

[6] `http://loc8.cc/ppg/pip`

Once you have `pip` installed, it is a simple matter to search for and install packages. Let's take an example: say we want to install *Sphinx*, the documentation generator we will use to document our plugins.

To install pip on Windows, see `http://www.pip-installer.org`

First let's find the package name using `pip`:

```
ophir:pyqgis gsherman$ pip search Sphinx
  Sphinx                  - Python documentation generator
  sphinxcontrib-blockdiag - Sphinx "blockdiag" extension
  sphinxcontrib-actdiag   - Sphinx "actdiag" extension
  dataflake.docbuilder    - Automated Sphinx documentation builder
  sphinxcontrib-nwdiag    - Sphinx "nwdiag" and "rackdiag" extension
  sphinxcontrib-seqdiag   - Sphinx "seqdiag" extension
```

This confirms that the package exists and we have the correct name. Installing it is simple:

```
ophir:pyqgis gsherman$ pip install sphinx
Downloading/unpacking sphinx
```

```
Downloading Sphinx-1.1.3.tar.gz (2.6MB): 2.6MB downloaded
Running setup.py egg_info for package sphinx

   no previously-included directories found matching 'doc/_build'
Downloading/unpacking Pygments>=1.2 (from sphinx)
   Downloading Pygments-1.6rc1.tar.gz (1.4MB): 1.4MB downloaded
   Running setup.py egg_info for package Pygments
   ...
Successfully installed sphinx Pygments docutils
Cleaning up...
```

Notice `pip` isn't case sensitive---it was happy to install Sphinx even though we used lower case in the install command. In addition to installing Sphinx, `pip` also installed two dependencies for us: `Pygments` and `docutils`.

[7] `pip freeze` generates a list suitable for a `requirements.txt` file which can be used by pip to install a set of packages using the `-r` or `--requirement` switch.

You can see which packages are installed on your system using `pip list`. Older versions of pip don't support the list command—in this case you can use `pip freeze` instead.[7]

Using `pip list` will generate an often lengthy list of all the packages installed on your system, along with the version number:

```
docutils (0.10)
docutils-ext (0.2d)
pdfrw (0.1)
pydns (2.3.6)
Pygments (1.6)
reportlab (2.7)
rst2pdf (0.93.dev)
see (1.0.1)
validate-email (1.1)
wsgiref (0.1.2)
```

2.6 Documenting Your Code

Documenting your code is important. Many a programmer has struggled to remember what they were thinking weeks or months ago when they wrote a chunk of code. In Python, documenting your code has the added advantage of making it available via the `help` function.

Remember our example *Point* class? If we import it and look at the help we get this:

```
>>> from point import Point
>>> help(Point)
```

```
class Point
 |  Methods defined here:
 |
 |  draw(self)
 |
 |  move(self, new_x, new_y)
 |
 |  ----------------------------------------
 |  Data and other attributes defined here:
 |
 |  marker_size = 4
```

This is nice, but it is also sparse. We see the methods and attributes defined but no description of what they actually do. Here is a new, documented version of our code:

Listing 2.4: point.py

```
1   class Point:
2       """ Class to model a point in 2D space."""
3
4       """ Size of our marker in pixels """
5       marker_size = 4
6
7       def draw(self):
8           """"Draw the point on the map canvas"""
9           print "drawing the point"
10
11      def move(self, new_x, new_y):
12          """ Move the point to a new location on the
13              map canvas"""
14          print "moving the point"
```

Now when we use the help function we can see our documentation for each method

```
>>> from point import Point
>>> help(Point)

Help on class Point in module point:

class Point
 |  Class to model a point in 2D space.
 |
 |  Methods defined here:
 |
 |  draw(self)
 |      Draw the point on the map canvas
```

```
|
|   move(self, new_x, new_y)
|       Move the point to a new location on the
|       map canvas
|
|   ----------------------------------------
|   Data and other attributes defined here:
|
|   marker_size = 4
```

This gives us more information about what each method does. Many documentation generators (for example, Sphinx) use these docstrings to generate a nicely formatted set of documentation for your code.

Keeping it Clean

As you write Python code, remember to keep it consistent and nicely formatted. One way is to use the pep8 tool to check your code. You can install pep8 using pip or easy_install. To use it, run it from the command line and pass the name of your Python script:

```
pep8 point.py
```

If you don't get any results, it means your code passes, otherwise a list of potential problems will be presented for you to consider and correct:

```
$ pep8 simplepoint.py
simplepoint.py:2:1: W293 blank line contains whitespace
```

This tells us there is an issue at line 2, column 1.

Many of the errors may seem inconsequential, but it doesn't hurt to keep your code as clean as possible. For more information on formatting your Python code, see the *Style Guide for Python Code*.[8]

[8] http://loc8.cc/ppg/pep8

2.7   Resources to Learn More

We've given you a very brief overview of the Python language to get you started. To learn more, here are a few free resources to help you with Python:

- *Dive Into Python* - available in a number of formats: http://www.diveintopython.net
- Official Python documentation: http://loc8.cc/ppg/py_2.7

- Python tutorial: `http://loc8.cc/ppg/py_tutorial`

In addition, there are a number of fine textbooks and tutorials available from your online or local bookseller.

In reality, you can get started with PyQGIS with a modicum of Python knowledge and pick up the rest along the way. Feel free to dig in and get started.

2.8   Exercises

1. Write a function to accept an x and y value and using string formatting, print it with a precision of four decimal places.

2. Call the function in exercise 1 using named parameters. Modify your function if needed.

3. Look at the output of *QgsPoint.wellKnownText()*, then modify our Point3D class so the output from the *wellKnownText* method includes the Z value.

3

Setting Up Your Development Tools

In order to develop PyQGIS scripts or plugins you need a proper development environment. For our purposes, this consists of:

1. Python 2.x

2. Integrated Development Environment (IDE) or a shell/editor combination

3. PyQt

4. Qt, including Designer

Let's look at each of these individually.

3.1 Python

Depending on your operating system, you may find that you already have Python installed.

Linux and Mac OS X

Python is usually installed as part of Linux and OS X. You can easily test this by opening a terminal or shell prompt and typing:

```
python
```

If Python is installed you will get version number and a prompt:

```
$ python
Python 2.7.2+ (default, Oct  4 2011, 20:06:09)
[GCC 4.6.1] on linux2
Type "help", "copyright", "credits" or "license" for more information.
>>>
```

If your version number is 2.x then you are set to go. If not, or attempting to run python gives an error, you'll have to install a proper version of Python. On Linux, use your package manager to locate and install Python. Mac OS X versions through Mavericks come with Python 2.x.

QGIS does not work with Python 3.x

Windows

Unless you build your own version of QGIS from source, you'll use either the Standalone or OSGeo4W installer.[9] This will provide you with a version of Python and associated libraries/modules that work with QGIS.

[9] http://loc8.cc/ppg/installer

When installing, do yourself a favor and choose a path that **doesn't** contain spaces to house your new QGIS installation. This will make setting up for your PyQGIS work much simpler.

If you are using Windows, installing QGIS using the OSGeo4W Installer will give you everything you need to develop with PyQGIS.

3.2   IDE or Editor

You have a choice when it comes to writing PyQGIS code. You can either use a text editor or an IDE. This topic has been the subject of many flame wars, but in the end it is a matter of personal preference. Using an IDE has advantages, especially when you are first getting acquainted with writing Python code. A good IDE can provide aids to help you navigate the code, display classes, methods, and attributes, and provide code completion for both Python and QGIS.

I use a mix of Vim and PyCharm for all my development.

Using an Editor

If you choose to use an editor, make sure you choose one that provides syntax highlighting and indentation for your code. Here are some of the free choices you might choose from:

- Vim - `http://www.vim.org`
- Emacs - `http://www.gnu.org/software/emacs`
- Notepad++ - `http://notepad-plus-plus.org`
- jEdit - `http://www.jedit.org`

There are a bunch of editors out there that will do the job. Choose one you are comfortable with and makes coding easier. For a comprehensive list, see the Python Wiki.[10]

[10] `http://loc8.cc/ppg/editors`

Using an IDE

While you can write code in an editor and debug it from a shell, an IDE can make the process easier, especially if you want to debug your plugin in QGIS. There are a lot of Python IDE's to choose from—some of them are free and others are not. Let's take a look at a couple of them.

PyDev

PyDev is a freely available IDE for developing with Python. Below you will find instructions for installing the Eclipse framework and PyDev.

1. Eclipse requires a Java Runtime Environment (JRE). If Java is not installed, go to `http://java.com` and follow the instructions to install the version appropriate for your operating system.

2. Download Eclipse from `http://eclipse.org/downloads`. You can choose either the Classic version or the IDE for Java Developers. There is no installer for Eclipse. Just unzip it into a directory of your choice.

3. Find the Eclipse executable in the unzipped directory and run it

4. From the Help menu, choose Install New Software

5. Click the *Add* button

6. In the *Add Repository* dialog, enter `Pydev and Pydev Extensions` for the Name and `http://pydev.org/updates` for the Location.

7. Click OK

8. Once the list is populated, click the checkbox next to PyDev and click the Next button

9. Click Next and follow the prompts to complete the install

10. Once the install is complete, you will be prompted to restart Eclipse

11. Once Eclipse restarts, open the PyDev perspective by choosing `Window->Open Perspective->Other` from the menu

12. Choose PyDev from the list and click OK

That's it—PyDev is now ready for use.

PyCharm

PyCharm is a full-featured commercial Python IDE. At version 3.0, there is a free community edition available with an impressive subset of features. The main thing lacking in the community edition is the ability to do remote debugging, a feature that can be tremendously helpful when writing plugins and standalone applications.

There are other free tools available for remote debugging that we'll look at in the chapter on Creating a Development Workflow, on page 153.

PyCharm also requires a fairly recent Java runtime. It is cross-platform and runs on Linux, Mac, and Windows.

PyCharm provides code completion for both PyQt and the QGIS modules, making it easier to get started writing code. It also has a Vim emulator for those of us that cherish that means of editing code.

As I said, there are a lot of other Python IDE's out there; some free and some not. For a fairly comprehensive collection, see the list on the Python Wiki.[11]

[11] http://loc8.cc/ppg/ide

3.3   Qt/PyQt

PyQt is the Python API interface to Qt, the C++ framework that QGIS is based on. Because QGIS is built on the Qt framework, we use PyQt when creating plugins to provide all the GUI elements we might need.

Installing PyQt

Depending on your platform, you may already have Qt and PyQt installed.

If you are using the Standalone or OSGeo4W Windows installers, you already have Qt and PyQt installed as part of the QGIS installation.

For Mac users, the Kyngchaos binaries include both the Qt and PyQt runtime libraries. If you want to create user interfaces using Qt Designer, you'll have to install the Qt Tools package that is part of the full Qt install for Mac.[12]

[12] http://download.qt-project.org

On Linux, you can use your package manager to install Qt and PyQt. If you want to develop user interfaces, be sure to get both the Qt and PyQt tools packages.

Next up, we'll look at the QGIS/Python "ecosystem" and how plugins work with QGIS.

4

The QGIS/Python Ecosystem

This chapter explains a bit of history and how Python and QGIS work together. You'll also learn how to manage Python plugins in QGIS.

4.1 History

Early in the development of QGIS, a plugin architecture was designed to provide a way to dynamically add new features and capabilities. This architecture was created using C++. Since writing a QGIS plugin in C++ is not a trivial task, the number of potential contributors was limited.

In 2007 work began to add Python as a scripting language. Python was chosen because it has become the *lingua franca* of the GIS scripting world and would integrate nicely with the QGIS API. When version 0.9 of QGIS was released in late 2007, it included support for writing scripts and plugins in Python.

With the first release of Python support, the number of contributed plugins grew at an exceptional rate, contributing to the overall growth of QGIS as a first-class desktop GIS.

4.2 How Python and QGIS work together

QGIS is written in C++ and is comprised of over 400 core classes that make up the application. Of these, roughly 75% are Python enabled through the use of SIP[13], the extension module generator that outputs C++ code. These

[13] http://loc8.cc/ppg/py_sip

"sip" files are compiled as part of QGIS to provide the Python interface to the classes. The Python support is divided into several modules:

- qgis.core - core classes
- qgis.gui - graphical user interface classes
- qgis.analysis - analysis related classes
- qgis.networkanalysis - classes for network analysis

Example Use of a QGIS Module

To use the QGIS classes in one of the modules, you simply import it in Python, then call the desired methods and/or access the attributes:

```
>>> from qgis.core import *
>>> v = QgsVectorLayer()
>>> v.setTitle('Sample Layer')
>>> v.title()
u'Sample Layer'
```

In this book, we'll focus on the use of the first two modules. As a PyQGIS developer, you generally don't need to be concerned about how the integration works; everything you need is built-in to your QGIS distribution.

4.3   Core versus Contributed plugins

QGIS plugins come in two flavors: C++ and Python. Writing a C++ plugin is considerably more complicated that writing one using PyQGIS—fortunately we're interested in the latter.

Plugins are categorized as either "core" or contributed plugins. Core plugins are part of the QGIS distribution and included when you install the application. These can be either C++ or Python plugins. Contributed plugins are written in Python and generally developed by the user community.

Contributed plugins can become core plugins if they are found to provide key functionality advantageous to the majority of QGIS users.

You can find and install contributed plugins from one or more *plugin repositories*.

4.4 Plugin Repositories

The QGIS project stores contributed Python plugins in a central repository located at `http://loc8.cc/ppg/plugins`. Some organizations maintain their own public repository, however, most developers are encouraged to submit their plugins to the official repository to make them easily discoverable.

Anyone can contribute a Python plugin to the official repository. Later we'll see how to build and package your plugin so it is ready to be shared with other QGIS users.

Although plugins can be installed manually, generally it is best to do so from within QGIS, as described in the next section.

4.5 Managing plugins

With the release of QGIS 2.0, the installation and management of Python plugins has been integrated into a single interface that provides a much improved user experience. The new manager is accessed from the `Plugins->Manage and Install Plugins...` menu.

Figure 4.1, on the next page, shows what the Plugin Manager looks like when first opened from the menu. The default view is a list of installed plugins, along with some management functions to enable/disable, upgrade, uninstall, and reinstall a plugin. Plugins that have a check mark are those that are currently enabled. Additionally, the right-panel gives you some information about the installed plugins and how to enable/disable them.

There are some important aspects to the list of installed plugins:

- Both Python and C++ plugins are listed
- Both core and contributed plugins are listed
- Core plugins cannot be uninstalled—the uninstall and reinstall plugin buttons are always disabled

You can distinguish between core and contributed plugins by examining the directory where each is installed. Core plugins are installed in the same directory as the QGIS application. Contributed (Python) plugins are installed in a subdirectory of your HOME directory (see Section 4.6, Python Plugin

Figure 4.1: Plugin Manager at Startup

Specifics, on page 46 for location on your operating system).

Installing Python Plugins

Plugins are installed using the *Plugin Manager*. When you first open the *Plugin Manager*, the configured repositories are queried and the list of plugins is updated and displayed by category: *Installed, Get more, Upgradeable*, and *Invalid*.

To install a new plugin, select *Get more* from the left panel and locate the plugin of interest in the list, highlight it, and click the *Install plugin* button to complete the install

Figure 4.2, on the next page shows the *Plugin Manager* ready to install the *PinPoint* plugin.

Use the *Search* box to narrow the list of plugins based on name, description, tags, or author.

Figure 4.2: Installing a Plugin with the Plugin Manager

Plugin Manager Options

Clicking *Settings* in the left panel of the *Plugin Manager* brings up the option panel shown in Figure 4.3, on the following page.

You can control how often QGIS checks for plugin updates by selecting an interval from the drop-down box.

Some plugins are tagged as experimental by their authors. This means they may not be ready for prime time, have an incomplete feature set, or may have bugs. You can choose to have these shown in the *Plugin Manager* by clicking the checkbox.

On the lower half of the settings panel you'll find the section that allows you to add repositories. Out of the box, QGIS has the master repository configured for you. If you need access to other repositories (such as one you set up for development purposes), add them to the list by giving them a name and the URL that points to the XML file describing the repository. We'll show you how to set up your own repository in Section 8.14, Setting Up a Repository, on page 115.

Figure 4.3: Plugin Manager Options

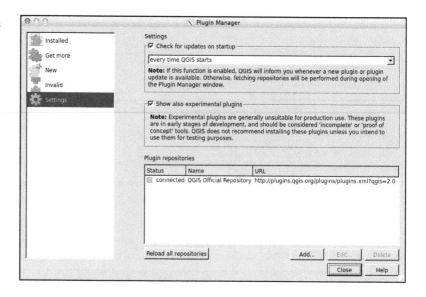

4.6 Python Plugin Specifics

Plugins you install using the *Python Plugin Installer* are downloaded from the repository as a zip file and extracted to a location that depends on your operating system:

- Linux: `.qgis2/python/plugins` in your home directory, typically found at `/home/gsherman/.qgis2/python/plugins`
- Mac OS X: `.qgis2/python/plugins` in your home directory, typically `/Users/gsherman/.qgis2/python/plugins`
- *Windows: `%HOMEDRIVE%\%HOMEPATH%\.qgis2\python\plugins`, by default:*

    - `C:\Documents and Settings\gsherman\.qgis2\python\plugins` on XP
    - `C:\Users\gsherman\.qgis2\python\plugins` on later versions

If you look in the `.qgis2/python/plugins` directory, you'll see a subdirectory for each plugin you have installed. It is possible to install plugins by simply downloading the zip file and unzipping it into your plugin directory. This can be helpful during development, however, generally you should use the *Plugin Manager* to manage your plugins. We'll take a look at development practices and how to package a plugin in Chapter 10, Writing Plugins, on page 131.

Now let's move on and take a look at navigating the QGIS API.

4.7   Exercises

1. Run QGIS and use the *Plugin Manager* to install the following plugins (we'll need them later on):

   a. ScriptRunner

   b. Plugin Builder

2. Determine where each plugin installed its menu.

3. Find each plugin's icon in the Plugins toolbar.

4. Use the *Plugin Manager* to disable *ScriptRunner* and note the changes to the menu and plugin toolbar.

5. Use your file manager or a command window to view the contents of your .qgis2/python/plugins directory and make note of the plugins you find there.

5

Navigating the QGIS API

Before we can really get into PyQGIS programming, we need a basic understanding of how to use both the QGIS and Qt API documentation. Since there are over 500 QGIS classes listed in the documentation, we obviously won't be going through them all. In this chapter we'll try to give you a broad overview, as well as specifics on how to decipher the documentation.

As we get into it, you'll notice the documentation is not Pythonic—it's C++. Return values, arguments, and definitions are based on C/C++ types and terminology. Sometimes this presents a bit of a problem when trying to interpret a particular class or method, but we'll work to make sense of it.

5.1   Finding the Documentation

The QGIS API documentation can be found at: `http://loc8.cc/ppg/api`. The documentation for Qt can be found at either `http://qt-project.org` or or `http://loc8.cc/ppg/pyqt_classes`. We'll primarily use the latter since it is specific to classes and methods supported by PyQt, however the official Qt documentation can also be quite useful as it often contains expanded explanations and examples.

5.2   A Simple Example

Let's start with a simple example using a QGIS class we are already somewhat familiar with—*QgsVectorLayer*.

The documentation for the constructor (the way we create the object) for *QgsVectorLayer* looks like this:

```
QgsVectorLayer (QString path=QString::null,
                QString baseName=QString::null,
                QString providerLib=QString::null,
                bool loadDefaultStyleFlag=true)
```

The QGIS API documentation is C++ centric, meaning all the types you'll see are C++ types. Don't worry, there are direct equivalents in Python that we'll point out.

First you'll notice the types specified are *QString* and bool. *QString* is a Qt class and bool is a C++ boolean type. Since C++ is *statically typed*, each argument, variable, and return value must have a type specified.

For comparison, here is how we would use *QgsVectorLayer* in Python:

```
layer = QgsVectorLayer('/data/alaska.shp', 'Alaska', 'ogr')
```

Since PyQt "maps" Python types to C++ types, we can just use Python strings to create the layer.

Python and C++ Types

Here are some Python equivalents to the Qt/C++ types you'll see in the API documentation:

Qt/C++	Python
QList, QSet, QVector	list
QMap	dict
QString	string
bool	bool

Notice we didn't specify a value of *loadDefaultStyleFlag*. In the documentation, any argument followed by an equal sign is optional. By not specifying *loadDefaultStyleFlag*, it defaulted to True. In fact, we can create a *QgsVectorLayer* without specifying any arguments:

```
layer = QgsVectorLayer()
```

This is because all of the arguments in the constructor are optional. Although we can create a layer in this manner, it isn't very useful:

```
>>> layer = QgsVectorLayer()
>>> layer.isValid()
False
```

Although *layer* is a valid object, it isn't a valid layer since no data source or provider was specified in its creation. Just because a constructor or method has default values doesn't mean we should always depend on them.

Let's take a look at another QGIS class: *QgsPoint*, which represents a simple 2D point. In the QGIS documentation, we find three ways to construct a point:

```
QgsPoint ()
QgsPoint (const QgsPoint &p)
QgsPoint (double x, double y)
```

The first method creates an "empty" point object at 0,0. The second creates a new point from an existing one, and the last creates a point from supplied x and y values:

```
>>> p1 = QgsPoint()
>>> p1
(0,0)
>>> p2 = QgsPoint(21.2, 100.9)
>>> p2
(21.2,100.9)
>>> p3 = QgsPoint(p2)
>>> p3
(21.2,100.9)
```

Now that we have a basic idea of how individual classes are documented, let's take a brief side trip into the world of signals and slots.

5.3   Signals and Slots

Qt uses the concept of signals and slots to communicate between objects. An object can raise a signal that can be received by a slot in another object. A concrete example will make this clearer.

Menu and toolbar items in Qt (and therefore QGIS) are usually created using a *QAction* object:

```
self.zoomin_action = QAction(
        QIcon(":/ourapp/zoomin_icon"),
        "Zoom In",
        self)
```

This creates an action with an icon and a text label of "Zoom In". An action must be added to a menu and/or toolbar before it is of any practical use.

If we look at the PyQt documentation for *QAction*[14], we find a number of signals associated with it:

- *changed()*
- *hovered()*
- *toggled(bool)*
- *triggered(bool = 0)*

[14] http://loc8.cc/ppg/pyqt_
qaction

Although the other signals may be of interest, in this example we will focus on the *triggered* signal. This signal is emitted when the user clicks on the menu item or toolbar button or presses the action's keyboard shortcut.

The emitted signal is of no use unless it is connected to a slot; a method that does something in response to the action being triggered. We connect our action to a slot like this:

```
self.zoomin_action.triggered.connect(self.zoom_in)
```

This means that when our *zoomin_action* is triggered, the zoom_in method (defined elsewhere in our code) will be called.

You can think of it as a listener that waits for a signal to be emitted and then does something in response. For an example of an action connected to a slot, see Section 12.4, Adding Map Tools to the Application, on page 168.

5.4   *The Layout of QGIS and PyQt Documentation*

The layout of QGIS and PyQt documentation is similar in form. Typically you will find these sections (among others) for a given class:

- Public Slots - methods we can connect to and/or override in our own subclass
- Signals - signals we can connect to slots
- Public Member Functions - functions/methods we can call
- Static Public Member Functions - functions/methods we can call without having an instance of the class
- Protected Member Functions - under C++, functions/methods accessible only by the class or subclasses, but accessible to us in Python

Let's look at a few of these sections from the documentation of *QgsVector-Layer* to get a better idea of how to use the API documentation.

Public Slots

QgsVectorLayer has a number of slots:

```
QgsGeometryCache * cache ()
void checkJoinLayerRemove (QString theLayerId)
    Check if there is a join with a layer that will be removed.
void deselect (const QgsFeatureId featureId)
    Deselect feature by its ID.
void deselect (const QgsFeatureIds &featureIds)
    Deselect features by their ID.
QString metadata ()
    Obtain Metadata for this layer.
virtual void onCacheImageDelete ()
    Is called when the cache image is being deleted.
void removeSelection ()
    Clear selection.
void select (const QgsFeatureId &featureId)
    Select feature by its ID.
void select (const QgsFeatureIds &featureIds)
    Select features by their ID.
void triggerRepaint ()
virtual void updateExtents ()
    Update the extents for the layer.
```

These are methods we can connect to from a *QAction* or some other Qt GUI element such as a drop-down box or checkbox.

While these are slots, they can be called like any other method in the class:

```
>>> lyr = QgsVectorLayer('/data/alaska.shp', 'Alaska', 'ogr')
>>> QgsMapLayerRegistry.instance().addMapLayer(lyr)
<qgis.core.QgsVectorLayer object at 0xc3b90bc>
>>> lyr.metadata()
u'<html><body><p class="subheaderglossy">General</p>\n<p
class="glossy">Storage type of this layer</p>\n<p>ESRI
Shapefile</p>\n<p class="glossy">Description of this
provider</p>\n<p>OGR data provider (compiled against GDAL/OGR
library version 1.10.0, running against GDAL/OGR library
version 1.10.0)</p>\n<p class="glossy">Source for this
layer</p>\n<p>/data/alaska.shp</p>\n<p
class="glossy">Geometry type of the features in this
layer</p>\n<p>Polygon</p>\n<p class="glossy">The number of
features in this layer</p>\n<p>653</p>\n<p
class="glossy">Editing capabilities of this layer</p>\n<p>Add
Features, Delete Features, Change Attribute Values, Add
```

```
Attributes, Delete Attributes, Create Spatial Index, Fast
Access to Features at ID, Change Geometries</p>\n<p
class="subheaderglossy">Extents</p>\n<p class="glossy">In
layer spatial reference system units</p>\n<p>xMin,yMin
-7115212.98,1368239.61 : xMax,yMax
4895579.81,7805331.22</p>\n<p class="glossy">Layer Spatial
Reference System</p>\n<p>+proj=aea +lat_1=55 +lat_2=65
+lat_0=50 +lon_0=-154 +x_0=0 +y_0=0 +datum=NAD27 +units=us-ft
+no_defs</p>\n</body></html>'
```

The *metadata()* method returns the metadata for our layer in HTML format.
If you were developing a plugin or standalone application and want to display the metadata for a layer in a *QTextBrowser* you could connect a button
click to the slot to fetch the HTML, then insert it into your *QTextBrowser*.

QTextBrowser:
http://loc8.cc/ppg/pyqt_qtb

If our plugin or application adds or removes features from the *QgsVector-Layer*, we would want to connect the *editingStopped* signal to the *updateExtents* slot. This would recalculate the extents based on the current features.

Signals

QgsVectorLayer has a fair number of signals; here a few of them from the
documentation:

```
void attributeAdded (int idx)
    Will be emitted, when a new attribute has been added to this
    vector layer.
void attributeDeleted (int idx)
    Will be emitted, when an attribute has been deleted from this
    vector layer.
void attributeValueChanged (QgsFeatureId fid, int idx, const QVariant &)
void beforeCommitChanges ()
    Is emitted, before changes are commited to the data provider.
void beforeRollBack ()
    Is emitted, before changes are rolled back.

...

void editingStarted ()
    Is emitted, when editing on this layer has started.
void editingStopped ()
    Is emitted, when edited changes successfully have been written
    to the data provider.
```

Any time you want to perform an action based on some event in your plugin
or application, you would connect one of these signals to the appropriate

method or function in your code.

As we illustrated in the previous example, we could connect the *editingStopped* signal to a function that calls the *updateExtents* slot to update the extents after changes have been made to the layer:

```
self.layer = QgsVectorLayer('/data/alaska.shp', 'Alaska', 'ogr')
self.layer.editingStopped.connect(self.update_our_extents)
...
def update_our_extents(self):
    self.layer.updateExtents()
```

This is a somewhat contrived example; typically when editing features through the QGIS interface this is done automatically.

Public Member Functions

QgsVectorLayer has a good number of public member functions (methods) that deal with adding/editing/deleting features and attributes, as well as rendering, selecting features, and returning information about the layer.

We won't list the methods here—just remember that when you want to know what a QGIS class can do, look at the public member functions.

Static Public Member Functions

Static functions or methods are different than the methods we've mentioned previously. Most of the methods require an *instance* of the class before you can access them. In this snippet of code, *layer* is the variable that holds an instance of *QgsVectorLayer*:

```
layer = QgsVectorLayer('/data/alaska.shp', 'Alaska', 'ogr')
```

In other words, we have created a *QgsVectorLayer* object by calling its constructor. Static methods don't use an instance—you call them directly referencing the class name.

Since the static method in *QgsVectorLayer* isn't very suitable for our example, let's illustrate using *QgsMessageLog*, a class that writes an entry to the *Log Messages* panel in QGIS. Here is a list of static methods available in *QgsMessageLog*:

You can access the Log Messages panel by clicking on the yellow triangle in the lower right of the status bar.

```
static QgsMessageLog *      instance ()
static void logMessage (QString message, QString tag=QString::null,
                         MessageLevel level=WARNING)
    add a message to the instance (and create it if necessary)
```

To log a message to the panel, we just use:

```
QgsMessageLog.logMessage('This is a warning---read carefully',
                         'Maps-be-us',
                         QgsMessageLog.WARNING)
```

You can give QgsMessageLog a try from the Python console in QGIS.

We don't need an instance of *QgsMessageLog* to use the method. We just supply our message, a tag that will be used as the tab name in the panel, and a message level.

Another example is the Qt class *QMessageBox*. If we look at the Qt documentation we find these public static methods:

```
void about ( QWidget * parent, const QString & title, const QString & text )
void aboutQt ( QWidget * parent, const QString & title = QString() )
StandardButton critical ( QWidget * parent, const QString & title,
                          const QString & text,
                          StandardButtons buttons = Ok,
                          StandardButton defaultButton = NoButton )
StandardButton information ( QWidget * parent, const QString & title,
                             const QString & text,
                             StandardButtons buttons = Ok,
                             StandardButton defaultButton = NoButton )
StandardButton question ( QWidget * parent, const QString & title,
                          const QString & text,
                          StandardButtons buttons = Ok,
                          StandardButton defaultButton = NoButton )
StandardButton warning ( QWidget * parent, const QString & title,
                         const QString & text,
                         StandardButtons buttons = Ok,
                         StandardButton defaultButton = NoButton )
```

Each of these methods can be used without creating a *QMessageBox* object. Some of the methods have optional values—remember any argument followed by an equal sign is optional. If you don't supply a value, the default is used.

For example, to create a simple "about" box we could use:

```
QMessageBox.about(
    None,
    'About MyPlugin',
```

```
'No animals were harmed in the development of this Plugin')
```

Which gives us the simple about box shown in Figure 5.1.

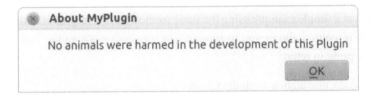

Figure 5.1: A Simple About Box using QMessageBox.about()

To display a warning message we could use:

```
QMessageBox.warning(
    None,
    'MyPlugin',
    'Warning, configuration file missing')
```

This static method gives us a little warning message as shown in Figure 5.2.

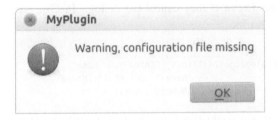

Figure 5.2: A warning message created with QMessageBox.warning()

Static public methods are quick and easy to use and you'll find them through-out both the QGIS and Qt API. Be sure to look through the API documentation for a class to familiarize yourself with the methods available.

5.5   *Choosing Between the Qt and PyQt Documentation*

You have two choices for documentation when working with the PyQt classes:

1. The official Qt documentation available at `http://loc8.cc/ppg/qt_doc`

2. The PyQt documentation at `http://loc8.cc/ppg/pyqt_doc`

Although the Qt documentation is perfectly usable, I suggest you use the PyQt version. If you compare, you'll find that often the return types are different between the two. This is because of the differences between C++ and Python. In C++ many of the methods "fill" a variable you provide to the method. In these situations, Python returns a tuple or a list.

Let's look at a simple example using the static method *getText* in *QInputDialog*. The *getText* method allows you to present a simple dialog box to the user and get a string in return.

Here is the documentation from the Qt site:

```
QString QInputDialog getText (QWidget *parent,
                              const QString  &title,
                              const QString  &label,
                              QLineEdit::EchoMode mode=QLineEdit::Normal,
                              const QString  &text=QString(),
                              bool  *ok=0,
                              Qt::WindowFlags flags=0)
```

If we provide the ok argument, *getText* will fill it with true if the user pushes the *OK* button and false if they cancel the dialog. In C++ we would do something like:

```
bool ok;
QString text = QInputDialog::getText(this, "Enter Your Name"),
                                    "Name:", QLineEdit::Normal,
                                    'Nobody', &ok);
```

When the dialog is closed, we could check to see if ok is true and then proceed to use the string returned in our text variable.

Now let's look at the PyQt documentation for *getText*:

```
(QString, bool ok) QInputDialog.getText (QWidget parent,
                              QString title
                              QString label
                              QLineEdit.EchoMode mode = QLineEdit.Norm
                              QString text = QString()
                              Qt.WindowFlags flags = 0)
```

Notice the return value. Instead of *getText* returning a string, it returns a tuple containing the user entered string (if any), and a boolean value indicating which button was clicked: True for *OK* or False for *Cancel*.

To use *getText* in Python, we would do something like this:

```
(name, ok) = QInputDialog.getText(None, "Enter Your Name",
                                  "Name:", QLineEdit.Normal,
                                  "Nobody")
```

When the method returns we check ok and determine what to do:

```
if ok:
    print "Thanks for the name: %s" % name
else:
    print "You cancelled your name input"
```

We could also just use the returned tuple:

```
the_result = QInputDialog.getText(None, "Enter Your Name",
                                  "Name:", QLineEdit.Normal,
                                  "Nobody")
if the_result[1]:
    print "Thanks for the name: %s" % the_result[0]
else:
    print "You cancelled your name input"
```

While this works, assigning the result to variables (name, ok) makes for code that is easier to read and understand.

Next we'll fire up the QGIS Python console and start using some of our PyQGIS skills.

6

Using the Console

The QGIS Python console is great for doing one-off tasks or experimenting with the API. Sometimes you might want to automate a task using a small script, and do it without writing a full blown plugin.

In this chapter we'll take a look at using the console to explore the workings of PyQGIS, as well as doing some real work.

6.1 Console Features and Options

Let's take a quick tour of the console features and options. With QGIS running, open the console using the Plugins->Python Console menu. Figure 6.1, on the following page shows the console right after opening it. Normally when you first open the console, it is docked near the bottom of the QGIS window; in our example, we have undocked it to make the window a little bigger.

The lower panel of the console is the input area; results of input are displayed in the upper panel.

On the left of the console you'll see a toolbar that contains the following tools, top to bottom:

Clear console: Clears the console of all previous commands and output

Import class: Import classes from the *processing*, *PyQt4.QtCore*, or

PyQt4.QtGui module by selecting one from the popup list

Run command: Run the current command in the input area

Show editor: Toggle the visibility of the editor

Settings: Configure the console behavior

Help: Open the help window for the console

Console Options

Clicking the *Settings* button brings up the console options dialog as shown in Figure 6.2, on the next page.

You can set the font for both the Console and the Editor, as well as enabling autocompletion. For the Editor, you can enable the object inspector which allows you to get a nice view of your code.

Lastly, you can choose to use the preloaded API files or untick the box and manually add your own. Generally you can stick with the preloaded files as they contain the information needed for autocompletion in the PyQt and QGIS API.

6.2   Using the Console Editor

The Console Editor provides an environment in which you can edit code, providing syntax highlighting and autocompletion. This can be useful for

Figure 6.2: Python Console Settings

writing concise scripts, prototyping, and testing. Usually you will want to use your favorite editor or IDE when working on a larger project.

Let's look at a few of the features found in the editor.

The Toolbar

The Console Editor toolbar is arranged vertically, with the following tools top to bottom:

Open file: Open a Python script located on disk. Multiple files can be opened, each assigned to a new tab.

Save: Save the edited script

Save As...: Save the current script to a file with a new name or location

Find Text: Search the current script for occurrences of a given text string

Cut: Cut the selected text to the clipboard

Copy: Copy the selected text to the clipboard

Paste: Paste the contents of the clipboard at the current cursor location

Comment: Comment out the current line or a selected set of lines

Uncomment: Uncomment the current line or a selected set of lines

Object Inspector: Open the object inspector to show a hierarchy of classes, methods, and functions in the current script

Run script: Run the current script in the console

Loading, Editing, and Running a Script

The `simple_point.py` script can be found in `http://locatepress.com/files/pyqgis_code.zip`, which includes all the code samples in the book.

Let's load the `simple_point.py` script that we looked at in Chapter 2, Python Basics, on page 17 and take a look at using it in the Console Editor.

Figure 6.3, on the next page shows our script loaded into the editor and the Object Inspector panel visible. Here's what we did to get to the point shown in the figure:

1. Open the Python Console

2. Click on the *Show Editor* button

3. Click *Open file* and load `simple_point.py`

4. Using the Editor, add the *my_function* function to the bottom of `simple_point.py`

5. Click *Save* to save the file

6. Open the Object Inspector and click the '+' to expand the *Point* node

7. Click the *Run script* button

8. Enter some commands in the console

```
>>> my_function()
```

```
'this does nothing'
>>> p = Point()
>>> p.draw()
drawing the point
>>> p.move(100, 100)
moving the point
```

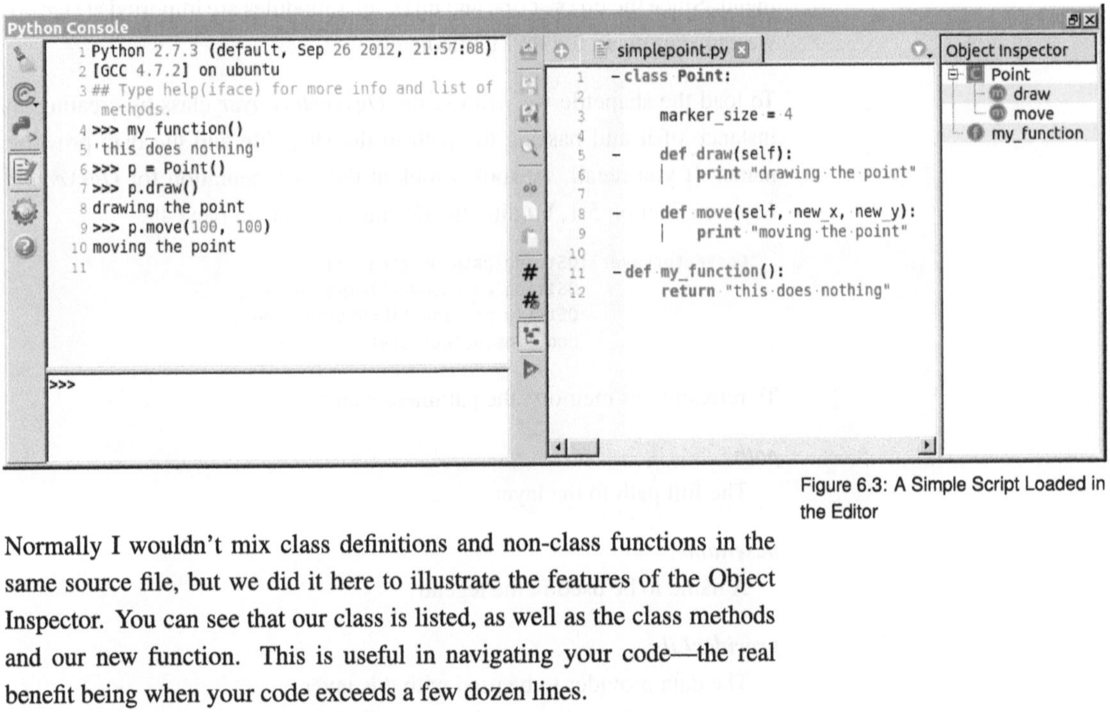

Figure 6.3: A Simple Script Loaded in the Editor

Normally I wouldn't mix class definitions and non-class functions in the same source file, but we did it here to illustrate the features of the Object Inspector. You can see that our class is listed, as well as the class methods and our new function. This is useful in navigating your code—the real benefit being when your code exceeds a few dozen lines.

When we click *Run script* in the Editor, it executes our code in the console. Since our code just defines a class and one function, there is no output in the console, however our class and function are now available for use.

In the console panel (left side), you can see the output from our commands. We'll take another look at this when we get to Section 7.1, Standalone Scripts in the Console, on page 73.

Now that we have an overview of the console and editor, let's put it to use. In the Introduction, we used the console to manipulate the map view in QGIS using methods exposed by the *qgis.util.iface* object. We'll take it a bit further now to actually load some data and work with the interface.

6.3   Loading a Vector Layer

To begin, let's load a shapefile into QGIS using the console. To do this, we will use the `world_borders.shp` shapefile from the sample dataset.

With QGIS running, open the console using the `Plugins->Python Console` menu. Since the `qgis.core` and `qgis.gui` modules are imported at startup, we can start using the API immediately.

To load the shapefile we will use the *QgsVectorLayer* class by creating an instance of it and passing the path to the shapefile and the data provider name. If you recall, we took a look at the documentation for *QgsVector-Layer* in Section 5.1, Finding the Documentation, on page 49:

```
QgsVectorLayer (QString path=QString::null,
                QString baseName=QString::null,
                QString providerLib=QString::null,
                bool loadDefaultStyleFlag=true)
```

To refresh your memory, the parameters are:

path:
   The full path to the layer

basename:
   A name to be used in the legend

providerLib:
   The data provider to be used with this layer

loadDefaultStyleFlag:
   Use the default style when rendering the layer. A style file has a `.qml` extension with same name as the layer and is stored in the same location.

First we create the layer in the console:

```
wb = QgsVectorLayer('/data/world_borders.shp', 'world_borders', 'ogr')
```

It is possible to create a vector layer that isn't valid. For example, we can specify a bogus path to a shapefile:

```
>>> bogus = QgsVectorLayer('/does/not/exist.shp', 'bogus_layer', 'ogr')
>>> bogus
<qgis.core.QgsVectorLayer object at 0x1142059e0>
```

Notice there is no complaint from QGIS, even though the shapefile doesn't exist. For this reason, you should always check the validity of a layer before adding it to the map canvas:

```
>>> bogus.isValid()
False
```

If the *isValid()* method returns False, there is something amiss with the layer and it can't be added to the map.

Getting back to our valid, world_borders layer, you'll notice nothing happened on the map canvas. We created a layer, however, for it to draw, we need to add to the list of map layers. To do this, we call a method in the *QgsMapLayerRegistry*:

```
QgsMapLayerRegistry.instance().addMapLayer(wb)
```

Once we do that, the layer is drawn on the map as shown in Figure 6.4.

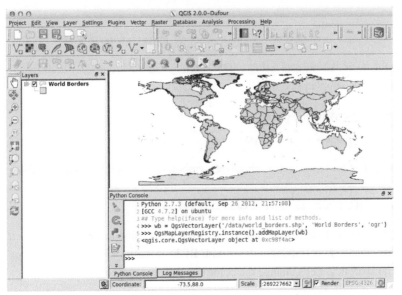

Figure 6.4: Using the Console to Load a Layer

Putting it all together, we have:

```
wb = QgsVectorLayer('/data/world_borders.shp', 'world_borders', 'ogr')
if wb.isValid():
    QgsMapLayerRegistry.instance().addMapLayer(wb)
```

If we want to remove the layer, we use the *removeMapLayer()* method and the layer id as an argument:

```
QgsMapLayerRegistry.instance().removeMapLayer(wb.id())
```

The layer is removed from both the map canvas and the legend, then the map is redrawn.

6.4   Exploring Vector Symbology

When you load a vector layer, it is rendered using a simple symbol and a random color. We can change the way a loaded layer looks by modifying the attributes of the symbol.

First let's load our `world_borders` layer:

```
>>> wb = QgsVectorLayer('/data/world_borders.shp', 'world_borders', 'ogr')
```

Next we get a reference to the renderer:[15]

```
>>> renderer = wb.rendererV2()
>>> renderer
<qgis.core.QgsSingleSymbolRendererV2 object at 0x114205830>
```

[15] Prior to version 2.0, QGIS had both a "new" and "old" rendering engine. In the API, the new is referred to as *V2*.

Our layer is rendered using a *QgsSingleSymbolRendererV2* which in our case, is a simple polygon fill.

To get the symbol, we use:

```
>>> symbol = renderer.symbol()
```

To get a bit of information about the symbol, we can use the *dump()* method:

```
>>> symbol.dump()
u'FILL SYMBOL (1 layers) color 134,103,53,255'
```

The output shows us that our layer is rendered using a fill symbol (which we already knew) using a color with RGB values of 134, 103, 53 and no transparency. Let's change the color to a dark red and refresh the map:

```
>>> from PyQt4.QtGui import QColor
>>> symbol.setColor(QColor('#800000'))
```

Let's analyze what we did here. To be able to change the color, we imported the QColor class from the PyQt4.QtGui module. The *setColor* method takes a *QColor* object as an argument.

QColor('#800000') creates a *QColor* object using a hex triplet string. When we pass this to *setColor* the fill color for our layer is set to a dark red. In Qt, there are many ways to create a *QColor*, including using twenty predefined colors that are accessible by name. Here are some ways you can create a valid *QColor*:

- QColor(Qt.red)
- QColor('red')
- QColor('#ff0000')
- QColor(255,0,0,255)

If you try the first method, you'll get an error because we haven't imported Qt. The fix is to import it prior to referencing *Qt.red*:

```
from PyQt4.QtCore import Qt
```

The last method is interesting in that it includes a value for the alpha-channel (transparency). Using this method of creating the color, we can also set the transparency of the layer. Each of these methods is described in the *QColor* documentation.

You'll notice that nothing happens on the map canvas when we change the color. We must tell QGIS to update the map canvas to reflect the changes to our layer:

```
>>> iface.mapCanvas().refresh()
```

This should redraw the map and our layer is now filled with a dark red color.

If nothing happened, it is likely you have render caching set to speed up map redraws. There are a couple of ways to deal with this—one is to always invalidate the cache prior to doing the refresh:

```
>>> wb.setCacheImage(None)
>>> iface.mapCanvas().refresh()
```

The other is to test to see if there is a cached image for the layer and, if so, invalidate it and then refresh:

```
>>> if wb.cacheImage() != None:
...     wb.setCacheImage(None)
...     iface.mapCanvas().refresh()
```

In practice, the first method should work in all situations, even if it is a bit "tacky" if render caching is not enabled.

Now that the layer is rendered in our new color, take a look at the legend—it still shows the previous color. To update it we need to call the *refreshLayerSymbology* method of the legend interface:

```
iface.legendInterface().refreshLayerSymbology(wb)
```

6.5   Loading a Raster Layer

Loading rasters is similar to loading a vector layer, except we use the *QgsRasterLayer* class:

```
QgsRasterLayer (const QString &path,
          const QString &baseName=QString::null,
          bool loadDefaultStyleFlag=true)
```

The parameters are the same as *QgsVectorLayer*, except we don't need to provide a data provider name---all rasters use GDAL.

In this example, we'll load `natural_earth.tif` raster into QGIS, display it, and then remove it using the console.

See `natural_earth.txt` in the sample data set for instructions on obtaining the Natural Earth raster.

To create the raster layer and add to the map, enter the following in the Python console:

```
>>> nat_earth = QgsRasterLayer('/data/natural_earth.tif',
... 'Natural Earth')
>>> QgsMapLayerRegistry.instance().addMapLayer(nat_earth)
<qgis.core.QgsRasterLayer object at 0x11483d8c0>
```

This creates the raster layer and adds it to *QgsMapLayerRegistry*. Note that the method used to add both vector and raster layers is the same: *addMapLayer*. We don't have to tell the registry what type of layer we are loading since *QgsVectorLayer* and *QgsRasterLayer* are both a "type" of *QgsMapLayer*.[16]

[16] In object oriented speak, they are child classes of QgsMapLayer.

Removing a raster layer is done the same way you remove a vector layer:

```
>>> QgsMapLayerRegistry.instance().removeMapLayer(nat_earth.id())
```

6.6   Data Providers

Since we've encountered data providers in the last couple of sections, it's worth explaining just a bit about them and their purpose. Simply put, QGIS uses data providers to interface with a data source. Data providers are written using a common specification, allowing QGIS to work with just about any spatial data store you can imagine. That's the good news---the sometimes bad news is they must be written in C++, not Python.

At present there are over ten data providers included with QGIS, covering a large portion of the data stores you will encounter, from file-based to relational databases.

You may be wondering what data providers are available and how you specify them when loading layers. The *QgsProviderRegistry* class is responsible for registering all the data providers when QGIS starts up—the *providerList()* method will return a list of all providers. From the console you can display all the available provider keys:

```
>>> for provider in QgsProviderRegistry.instance().providerList():
...     print provider
WFS
delimitedtext
gdal
gpx
memory
mssql
ogr
osm
postgres
spatialite
sqlanywhere
wms
```

In QGIS, you can use the *Providers* tab in the *About* dialog to view a description of all the available providers. The list of provider keys above corresponds to:

- WFS data provider
- Delimited text data provider
- GDAL provider
- GPS eXchange format provider

- Memory provider
- MSSQL spatial data provider
- OGR data provider (compiled against GDAL/OGR library version 1.9.1, running against GDAL/OGR library version 1.9.1)
- Open Street Map data provider
- PostgreSQL/PostGIS data provider
- SpatiaLite data provider
- SQL Anywhere data provider
- OGC Web Map Service version 1.3 data provider

Now that we have some experience with the console, let's move on to running scripts using a couple of different methods.

6.7   Exercises

1. Using the console, add the world borders layer to the map canvas, then:

2. Change the color to green with 50% transparency

3. Update the layer and legend

7

Running Scripts

PyQGIS scripts are a good way to perform tasks within QGIS without resorting to writing a plugin. It's easy to integrate scripts into your workflow and use them to load and style layers, manipulate the map view, and control a lot of QGIS functionality.

In this chapter we'll take a look at running standalone scripts and then use both the Python Console and the *Script Runner* plugin to load, manage, and run our scripts.

7.1 Standalone Scripts in the Console

We have seen how to execute Python statements in the console by typing them in one at a time, or perhaps by pasting from another source. This is a great way to explore the API, but is tedious when you are trying to do repetitive or complicated tasks. To get started, we'll write a script to perform some of the tasks we did interactively in Section 1.5, Your First PyQGIS experiment, on page 13 and in Chapter 6, Using the Console, on page 61.

The tasks we want to perform are:

1. Load the `world_borders` layer

2. Get the active layer

3. Change the color of the layer

4. Update the legend

5. Open the attribute table

Writing a Simple Script

Our task list may look a bit ambitious, however it won't take much code to accomplish:

Listing 7.1: first_script.py

```
1   from PyQt4.QtGui import *
2   from PyQt4.QtCore import *
3   from qgis.core import *
4   from qgis.utils import iface
5
6
7   def load_layer():
8       wb = QgsVectorLayer('/data/world_borders.shp', 'world_borders', 'ogr')
9       QgsMapLayerRegistry.instance().addMapLayer(wb)
10
11
12  def change_color():
13      active_layer = iface.activeLayer()
14      renderer = active_layer.rendererV2()
15      symbol = renderer.symbol()
16      symbol.setColor(QColor(Qt.red))
17      iface.mapCanvas().refresh()
18      iface.legendInterface().refreshLayerSymbology(active_layer)
19
20
21  def open_attribute_table():
22      iface.showAttributeTable(iface.activeLayer())
```

Let's take a look at how this script works. In *lines 1 through 4* we import the modules we'll need. When writing anything other than a trivial script, you'll find you usually need to import *PyQt4.QtCore*, *PyQt4.QtGui*, *qgis.core*, and *qgis.gui*. In this case we didn't need the *qgis.gui* module. We also imported *qgis.utils.iface* since it provides access to some of the functions we'll need.

Depending on how we run our script, we may not need the qgis.utils.iface import. If executed from the Python console editor, the import is not needed. To make the script flexible, it's best to include it.

The script is divided into three methods that do the work:

- *load_layer*
- *change_color*

- *open_attribute_table*

All of the methods used in the script were explained in the previous chapters, so let's look at how to actually run this script in the QGIS Python console.

The first thing we need to do is make sure QGIS (and Python) can find our script. If you load and run your script from the editor you don't have to worry about setting the path, however, you may want to run scripts from the console prompt. In this case, there are a number of ways to set the path:

1. Interactively add it to *sys.path* in the console

2. Add the path to the script to the PYTHONPATH environment variable

3. Permanently add the path using the Settings->Options->System menu

Let's say we typically store our scripts in a directory named pyqgis_scripts. For this example we'll assume this is found in the following locations, depending on your operating system:

- Linux: /home/gsherman/pyqgis_scripts
- Mac: /Users/gsherman/pyqgis_scripts
- Windows: C:/pyqgis_scripts

Let's take a look at each of these methods and see how we might use them.

In the QGIS Python Console, on Linux, we do the following to get access to our script:

```
>>> import sys
>>> sys.path.append('/home/gsherman/pyqgis_scripts')
>>> import first_script
>>> first_script.load_layer()
>>> first_script.change_color()
>>> first_script.open_attribute_table()
```

If we want to run this on Windows, the only difference is the append statement:

```
>>> sys.path.append('C:/pyqgis_scripts')
```

To use the PYTHONPATH environment variable, point it at the appropriate path for your operating system. This must be done prior to running QGIS. On Linux and Mac, you can do it manually each time using a shell script or you could add it to your login .profile or .bash_profile. On Windows the easiest way is to permanently add it to your environment settings.

With PYTHONPATH set, our console session looks like this:

```
>>> import first_script
>>> first_script.load_layer()
>>> first_script.change_color()
>>> first_script.open_attribute_table()
```

The last way to point to our code is to permanently set PYTHONPATH in QGIS using Settings->Options->System as seen in Figure 7.1. Here we added the path and selected the Append option so as not to destroy any existing PYTHONPATH settings. A restart of QGIS is required for the setting to take effect. With it in place, we can run the script exactly like we did in the previous example where we set PYTHONPATH in our environment.

Figure 7.1: Permanently Adding a PYTHONPATH

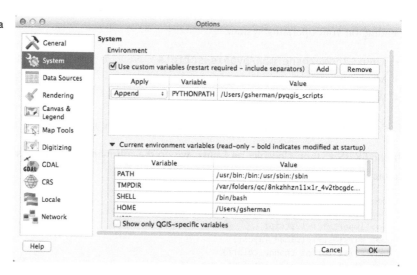

If you get errors when importing your script, check to make sure you have the path to pyqgis_scripts specified correctly in either *sys.path*, the PYTHONPATH environment variable, or the QGIS options setting.

When you call each of the methods in our script, you'll see that the world_borders
layer is added to the map, the color is changed to red and the legend is updated. The last method opens the attribute table for our layer.

We could have chosen to combine the *load_layer* and *change_color* methods into one, or even call *change_color* from the *load_layer* method. In
fact, the script doesn't have to use any methods at all. We could just do the
imports and then execute all the statements:

Listing 7.2: no_methods.py

```
1   from PyQt4.QtGui import *
2   from PyQt4.QtCore import *
3   from qgis.core import *
4   from qgis.utils import iface
5
6   wb = QgsVectorLayer('/data/world_borders.shp', 'world_borders', 'ogr')
7   QgsMapLayerRegistry.instance().addMapLayer(wb)
8
9   active_layer = iface.activeLayer()
10  renderer = active_layer.rendererV2()
11  symbol = renderer.symbol()
12  symbol.setColor(QColor(Qt.red))
13  iface.mapCanvas().refresh()
14  iface.legendInterface().refreshLayerSymbology(active_layer)
15
16  iface.showAttributeTable(iface.activeLayer())
```

Notice we have removed the method definitions; everything else remains
the same. When we import this script, it executes all the code immediately.
At times you may find this method of running a script fits your needs.

Rewriting the Script Using a Class

We can make our script a bit more elegant by refactoring it into a Python
class. This allows us to persist data during the lifetime of the class and
makes the code more friendly. The method(s) of setting the Python path
remain the same, but the way in which we use the class to execute the code
is a bit different. Here is the original script, refactored into a class:

Listing 7.3: first_script_class.py

```
1   from PyQt4.QtGui import *
2   from PyQt4.QtCore import *
3   from qgis.core import *
```

```
4
5
6   class FirstScript:
7
8       def __init__(self, iface):
9           self.iface = iface
10
11      def load_layer(self):
12          wb = QgsVectorLayer('/data/world_borders.shp', 'world_borders', 'ogr')
13          QgsMapLayerRegistry.instance().addMapLayer(wb)
14
15      def change_color(self):
16          active_layer = self.iface.activeLayer()
17          renderer = active_layer.rendererV2()
18          symbol = renderer.symbol()
19          symbol.setColor(QColor(Qt.red))
20          self.iface.mapCanvas().refresh()
21          self.iface.legendInterface().refreshLayerSymbology(active_layer)
22
23      def open_attribute_table(self):
24          self.iface.showAttributeTable(self.iface.activeLayer())
```

Let's take a look at the class to see how it's different from our original
script. First, notice that we have added a new method named _init_. This
method is called when you create an instance of a class. Since a reference to
qgis.utils.iface is passed and stored (*self.iface* in *line 9*), we no longer need
to import *iface* from *qgis.utils*. Now when a new instance of *FirstScript* is
created, we have access to the *iface* attribute:

```
>>> fs = FirstScript(qgis.utils.iface)
>>> fs.iface
<qgis.gui.QgisInterface object at 0x1130d0440>
```

For an explanation of the use of self,
see http://loc8.cc/ppg/self

The remaining methods in our class look similar to those in the original
script, except each is defined with a *self* argument as seen in *lines 11, 15,
and 23* of first_script_class.py. This is the standard way of defining class methods. The other difference is, we use *self.iface* to access the
activeLayer, *refreshLayerSymbology*, and *showAttributeTable* methods.

Using our class, the console session looks like this:

```
>>> from first_script_class import FirstScript
>>> fs = FirstScript(qgis.utils.iface)
>>> fs.load_layer()
>>> fs.change_color()
>>> fs.open_attribute_table()
```

This provides us with a bit cleaner and more object oriented approach to our script.

7.2   Running Scripts with Script Runner

Running a script in the console is a decent way to work with PyQGIS. In this section we'll look at an alternative way to manage, view, and run your scripts using the *Script Runner* plugin.

If you did the exercises back in Chapter 4, The QGIS/Python Ecosystem, on page 41, you already have *Script Runner* installed. If not, install it now using the plugin installer by clicking on the Plugins->Manage and Install Plugins menu.

Figure 7.2 shows the *Script Runner* plugin after you first start it up.

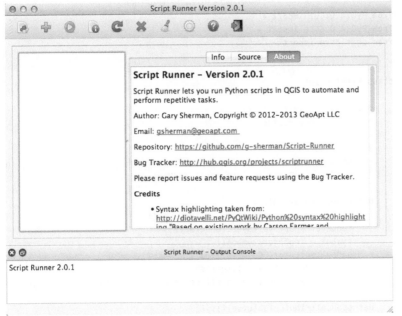

Figure 7.2: The Script Runner Plugin at Startup

To run an existing script, you first add it to Script Runner using the *Add Existing Script* tool on the toolbar. This will add it to a list in the left panel and *Script Runner* will remember the next time you start it up. You can remove a script using the *Remove Script* tool. This just removes it from the list; it does nothing to the script file on disk.

Once you have a script loaded, you can click the *Script Info* tool to populate the Info and Source tabs in the panel on the right. The Info tab contains the *docstring* from your module and a list of the classes, methods, and functions found in the script. Having a proper docstring at the head of each script will help you easily determine its purpose. You can view the source of the script on the Source tab. This allows you to quickly confirm that you are using the right script.

Scripts managed by *Script Runner* have only one mandatory requirement—they must implement a *run_script* method that accepts a single argument. This is the only thing we have to add to our *FirstScript* class to make it run inside *Script Runner*:

Listing 7.4: first_script_sr.py

```
1   from PyQt4.QtGui import *
2   from PyQt4.QtCore import *
3   from qgis.core import *
4
5
6   class FirstScript:
7
8       def __init__(self, iface):
9           self.iface = iface
10
11      def load_layer(self):
12          wb = QgsVectorLayer('/data/world_borders.shp', 'world_borders', 'ogr')
13          QgsMapLayerRegistry.instance().addMapLayer(wb)
14
15      def change_color(self):
16          active_layer = self.iface.activeLayer()
17          renderer = active_layer.rendererV2()
18          symbol = renderer.symbol()
19          symbol.setColor(QColor(Qt.red))
20          self.iface.mapCanvas().refresh()
21          self.iface.legendInterface().refreshLayerSymbology(active_layer)
22
23      def open_attribute_table(self):
24          self.iface.showAttributeTable(self.iface.activeLayer())
25
26
27  def run_script(iface):
28      fs = FirstScript(iface)
29      fs.load_layer()
30      fs.change_color()
```

31   `fs.open_attribute_table()`

Lines 27-31 define the *run_script* method. Notice it accepts a reference
to the *qgis.utils.iface* class and we pass that along when we instantiate
FirstScript (*line 28*).

Note that the *run_script* method is not indented the same as the other methods and is **not** part of the *FirstScript* class.

We can now add our script to *Script Runner* by clicking the Add Script
button and choosing it from our scripts directory. Once it is added, click
on the Info tab to get some basic information about the script as shown in
Figure 7.3.

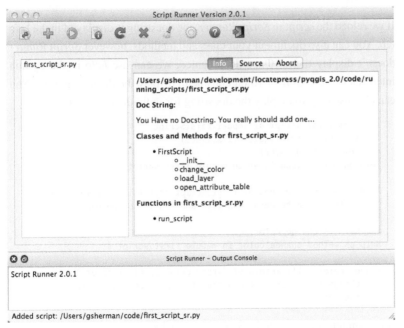

Figure 7.3: Script Information in Script Runner

Notice that it tells us we have no Docstring and we "really should add one."
Let's learn how to fix that now.

Adding Code Documentation

A docstring is used by Python to document your modules, classes, and methods. This information is also displayed when you use the *help* function in the Python console. Documenting your code is easy—you just add single or multi-line strings to your classes and methods right in your source code. For example, to document our *FirstScript* class, we add the following docstring to the beginning of the script:

```
"""FirstScript: A simple class used to load a layer in QGIS
and change its color."""

from PyQt4.QtGui import *
from PyQt4.QtCore import *
from qgis.core import *


class FirstScript:
    ...
```

If we reload the script in *Script Runner*, the docstring is displayed in the Info tab. You can also document your class and methods, however *Script Runner* doesn't display them. Once documented, we can use *help* in the Python interpreter or the QGIS Python console to display the documentation. You can also use *help* to display the docstring for individual methods:

```
>>> from first_script_sr import FirstScript
>>> fs = FirstScript(qgis.utils.iface)
>>> help(fs.load_layer)
Help on method load_layer in module first_script_sr:

load_layer(self) method of first_script_sr.FirstScript instance
    Load the world_borders shapefile and add it to the map.

>>> help(fs.change_color)
Help on method change_color in module first_script_sr:

change_color(self) method of first_script_sr.FirstScript instance
    Change the color of the active layer to red and update
    the legend.
```

Our complete, documented script now looks like this:

Listing 7.5: first_script_sr_documented.py

```
1  """FirstScript: A simple class used to load a layer in QGIS
2  and change its color."""
```

```
 3
 4   from PyQt4.QtGui import *
 5   from PyQt4.QtCore import *
 6   from qgis.core import *
 7
 8
 9   class FirstScript:
10       """Class to load and render the world_borders shapefile."""
11
12       def __init__(self, iface):
13           self.iface = iface
14
15       def load_layer(self):
16           """Load the world_borders shapefile and add it to the map."""
17           wb = QgsVectorLayer('/data/world_borders.shp', 'world_borders', 'ogr')
18           QgsMapLayerRegistry.instance().addMapLayer(wb)
19
20       def change_color(self):
21           """Change the color of the active layer to red and update
22           the legend."""
23           active_layer = self.iface.activeLayer()
24           renderer = active_layer.rendererV2()
25           symbol = renderer.symbol()
26           symbol.setColor(QColor(Qt.red))
27           self.iface.mapCanvas().refresh()
28           self.iface.legendInterface().refreshLayerSymbology(active_layer)
29
30       def open_attribute_table(self):
31           """Open the attribute table for the active layer."""
32           self.iface.showAttributeTable(self.iface.activeLayer())
33
34
35   def run_script(iface):
36       """Run the script by instantiating FirstScript and calling
37       methods."""
38       fs = FirstScript(iface)
39       fs.load_layer()
40       fs.change_color()
41       fs.open_attribute_table()
```

Advantages of Using Script Runner

You may have realized that using *Script Runner* has several advantages. For one, we don't have to fiddle with our Python path to run our script. *Script Runner* takes care of all that once you add a script. Additionally, having all your scripts organized in a neat list is handy, regardless of where they are actually located on disk. The information and source viewing features of the plugin are also useful.

Best of all, enabling an existing script to work with *Script Runner* is a simple matter of adding the *run_script* method, creating an instance of your class, then calling one or more methods to do the job.

In the next chapter we'll take a look at a number of tips and techniques you will find useful when working with PyQGIS.

7.3   Exercises

1. The `first_script.py` script doesn't check to see if the data layer is valid. Modify `first_script.py` to implement this check and handle any failures gracefully. Test your changes in the console.

2. Modify the *change_color* method in the *FirstScript* class to accept a color value instead of defaulting to *Qt.red*. Your change should allow specifying a color value using named colors, RGBA values, and hex color notation. Test your changes in the console.

3. Modify the *load_layer* method in *FirstScript* to accept a user-specified layer name and path instead of loading the `world_borders` layer. Test your changes in the console.

4. Create a new script to run in *Script Runner* with a single method *load_raster* that loads the Natural Earth raster. Run the script and ensure that it properly loads the raster.

8

Tips and Techniques

This chapter provides examples of common, and some perhaps, unique techniques you will find helpful when working with PyQGIS. The QGIS API documentation will come in very handy as you work with various aspects of the interface.[17]

Many more examples can be found in the PyQGIS Cookbook.[18]

[17] QGIS API: http://loc8.cc/ppg/api
[18] http://loc8.cc/ppg/cookbook

8.1   *Loading Vector Layers*

QGIS supports a wide range of data stores for vector layers. This section gives you a few examples of loading layers and displaying them on the map canvas.

OGR Layers

In Chapter 6, Using the Console, on page 61 we saw a complete example of loading a vector layer using the `QgsVectorLayer` class:

```
wb = QgsVectorLayer('/data/world_borders.shp', 'world_borders', 'ogr')
QgsMapLayerRegistry.instance().addMapLayer(wb)
```

This creates a layer from a shapefile and adds it to the map. Here are details:

imports:
   qgis.core

classes:
> QgsMapLayerRegistry, QgsVectorLayer

provider:
> OGR

This example will work with any OGR supported layer. For example, we can load a GML layer using:

```
gml_lyr = QgsVectorLayer('/data/qgis_sample_data/gml/lakes.gml',
                         'lakes',
                         'ogr')
QgsMapLayerRegistry.instance().addMapLayer(gml_lyr)
```

In our example, the *QgsVectorLayer* constructor takes three arguments:

- Full path to the data file: *'/data/qgis_sample_data/gml/lakes.gml'*
- A name to be used in the legend: *'lakes'*
- The provider name: *'ogr'*

Memory Layers

QGIS also supports what's known as a *memory* layer which can be very useful when writing plugins and scripts. A *memory* layer doesn't exist on disk and disappears when QGIS exits, but behaves like any other vector layer. If needed, a *memory* layer can be saved to disk in any format supported by QGIS.

There are two ways to create a memory layer:

1. Create the layer using *QgsVectorLayer*, specifying *memory* as the provider, then:[19]

- Get the reference to the provider
- Add each attribute needed by creating *QgsField* objects

[19] This method is illustrated in the PyQGIS Cookbook: `http://loc8.cc/ppg/cookbook`.

2. Use a URI that specifies the coordinate system, geometry type, and the fields to create the layer

The second method is much quicker and easier to use because we can specify the coordinate system (CRS) and the fields all at once:

You can create memory layers containing other geometry types, including `Point`, `MultiLineString`, and `Polygon`.

```
mem_layer = QgsVectorLayer(
    "LineString?crs=epsg:4326&field=id:integer"
```

```
"&field=road_name:string&index=yes",
"Roads",
"memory")
```

This creates a linestring memory layer with two fields (id and road_name) using the WGS84 coordinate system. We also included the *'index=yes'* keyword which tells the provider to create a spatial index for the features.

We add this to QGIS using the console:

```
QgsMapLayerRegistry.instance().addMapLayer(mem_layer)
```

If we open the layer properties dialog and look at the *Fields*, we can see the results as shown in Figure 8.1.

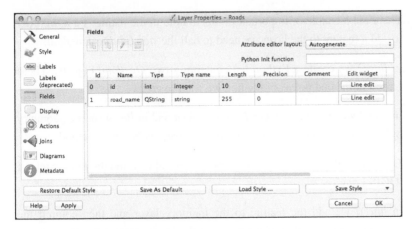

Figure 8.1: Fields in the Memory Layer

Looking at the *Metadata* also confirms that our layer was created successfully:

- **Storage type of this layer**: Memory storage
- **Description of this provider**: Memory provider
- **Source for this layer**: LineString?crs=epsg:4326&field=id:integer&field=road_name:string&index=yes
- **Geometry type of the features in this layer**: Line
- **The number of features in this layer**: 0
- **Editing capabilities of this layer**: Add Features, Delete Features, Change Attribute Values, Add Attributes, Delete Attributes, Create Spatial Index, Fast Access to Features at ID, Change Geometries
- **Extents in layer spatial reference system units**: unknown extent

- **Layer Spatial Reference System**: +proj=longlat +datum=WGS84 +no_defs

Our new memory layer fully supports editing of both features, attributes, and geometries. Since we just created it, there are no features and QGIS reports the extent as unknown.

We can add a feature to the layer in just a few steps:

```
1    mem_layer.startEditing()
2    points = [QgsPoint(-150, 61), QgsPoint(-151, 62)]
3    feature = QgsFeature()
4    feature.setGeometry(QgsGeometry.fromPolyline(points))
5    feature.setAttributes([1, 'QGIS Lane'])
6    mem_layer.addFeature(feature, True)
7    mem_layer.commitChanges()
```

There are a couple of important points to note in the listing. First, in order to add a feature to the layer we need to call the *startEditing()* method.

In *line 2* we create a Python list containing two *QgsPoint* objects. These represent the end points of the line we want to create.

In *line 3* we create a new *QgsFeature* object and in *line 4* set the geometry by passing the *points* list to the *QgsGeometry.fromPolyline* method.

Line 5 adds the attributes for our new feature: id of 1 and the *road_name* of 'QGIS Lane'.

In *line 6* we add the feature to the memory layer and then commit the changes in *line 7*. Now if we zoom to the layer extent we will see a single road. Opening the attribute table confirms that the feature was created and the attributes properly added.

Using iface to Load Layers

From a plugin or the console, you can add both vector and raster layers using *iface* methods (*addVectorLayer* and *addRasterLayer*). For example:

```
lyr = iface.addVectorLayer('towns.shp', 'towns', 'ogr')
```

Using this method saves you a step; the layer is added to the map without having to call *QgsMapLayerRegistry.instance().addMapLayer()*. In our examples, we used the two step method to help you understand the process. **When developing a standalone application using the QGIS API, you won't have access to the *iface* object.**

8.2   Loading Raster Layers

Loading a raster layer requires only the full path to the raster and a name of your choosing to be displayed in the legend:

```
raster_lyr = QgsRasterLayer('/data/qgis_sample_data/raster/landcover.img',
                            'Land Cover')
QgsMapLayerRegistry.instance().addMapLayer(raster_lyr)
```

As mentioned in the previous section, we could accomplish the same using *iface*:

```
raster_lyr = iface.addRasterLayer('/data/qgis_sample_data/raster/landcover.img',
                                  'Land Cover')
```

8.3   Working with Databases

Adding a PostgreSQL/PostGIS Layer

The easiest way to figure out how to add a PostGIS layer is to add it using the QGIS interface, then look at the connection information in the Metadata tab of the layer properties dialog. This will give you all the parameters needed to make a successful connection and add a layer.

Here is an example of loading a PostGIS layer.

```
db_lyr = QgsVectorLayer("dbname='gis_data' host=localhost port=5432 "
                        "srid=4326 type=MULTILINESTRING "
```

```
            "table='public'.'streets' (the_geom) sql=",
            'streets3',
            'postgres')
```

Though we formatted it to make it more readable, the first argument consists of a single concatenated string which tells QGIS how to access the layer:

```
"dbname='gis_data' host=localhost port=5432 "
"srid=4326 type=MULTILINESTRING "
"table='public'.'streets' (the_geom) sql="
```

When we added disk-based layers (e.g. shapefile, GML), we used the full path to the layer—the three lines above do the same for our database layer. The remaining arguments are streets3, the name that will appear in the legend, and postgres, the provider key.

Using an Existing PostgreSQL Connection

Sometimes you may want to send SQL to your PostgreSQL database from a plugin or PyQGIS script. To do this, you need a connection to your database. Since QGIS uses its own low-level interface to PostgreSQL, it can't provide a connection for general query use. You can, however, use the information from the QGIS PostgreSQL data provider to create your own connection using *QSqlDatabase*, a Qt class.

You could use *QSettings* to read the stored connection information from your settings, but this may not always work if the password isn't stored with the connection.

Here is an example that uses the active layer in QGIS to get the connection parameters, create a connection, and execute a query that returns some data:

```
1    """Use the database provider to connect to PostgreSQL.
2    This script is set up to run under the Script Runner plugin, but
3    can be also be run from the Python console.
4    """
5
6    from PyQt4.QtCore import *
7    from PyQt4.QtGui import *
8    from PyQt4.QtSql import *
9
10   from qgis.core import *
11
12
13   def run_script(iface):
```

```
14      # get the active layer
15      layer = iface.activeLayer()
16      # get the underlying data provider
17      provider = layer.dataProvider()
18      if provider.name() == 'postgres':
19          # get the URI containing the connection parameters
20          uri = QgsDataSourceURI(provider.dataSourceUri())
21          print uri.uri()
22          # create a PostgreSQL connection using QSqlDatabase
23          db = QSqlDatabase.addDatabase('QPSQL')
24          # check to see if it is valid
25          if db.isValid():
26              print "QPSQL db is valid"
27              # set the parameters needed for the connection
28              db.setHostName(uri.host())
29              db.setDatabaseName(uri.database())
30              db.setPort(int(uri.port()))
31              db.setUserName(uri.username())
32              db.setPassword(uri.password())
33              # open (create) the connection
34              if db.open():
35                  print "Opened %s" % uri.uri()
36                  # execute a simple query
37                  query = db.exec_("""select * from qgis_sample.airports
38                      order by name""")
39                  # loop through the result set and print the name
40                  while query.next():
41                      record = query.record()
42                      print record.field('name').value().toString()
43              else:
44                  err = db.lastError()
45                  print err.driverText()
```

Another approach is to use the psycopg2[20] Python module to create a connection using the data source URI of the active layer.

[20] http://loc8.cc/ppg/psycopg2

8.4   Working with Symbology

QGIS has sophisticated symbology capabilities. In this section we have a few simple examples of working with symbology. For additional examples, see the PyQGIS Cookbook[21]

[21] http://loc8.cc/ppg/cookbook

Simple Symbology

We have seen examples of working with symbols in Chapter 7, Running Scripts, on page 73 and Chapter 6, Using the Console, on page 61. Given a reference to a layer (layer), we can change the look in the following ways:

```
renderer = layer.rendererV2()
symbol = renderer.symbol()
symbol.setColor(QColor(Qt.Red))
symbol.setColor(QColor('red'))
symbol.setColor(QColor('#ff0000'))
symbol.setColor(QColor(255, 0, 0, 255))
```

Each of the setColor statements above will set the symbol color to red. After setting the color we must refresh the map canvas and the legend:

```
iface.mapCanvas().refresh()
iface.legendInterface().refreshLayerSymbology(layer)
```

Setting Transparency

You can set the transparency using setAlpha:

```
symbol.setAlpha(0.5)
```

This sets the transparency for the symbol to 50%. Be sure to refresh the canvas and legend after making changes.

Customizing Symbols

For each symbol type (marker, line, fill) we can set additional properties to control the appearance using the createSimple method. This method is available for:

- *QgsMarkerSymbolV2*
- *QgsLineSymbolV2*
- *QgsFillSymbolV2*

The createSimple method uses keywords in a dictionary to define the appearance of the new symbol. The keywords for each symbol type are listed below.

Keywords and values for QgsMarkerSymbolV2:

angle
    Specified in radians

color
   Specified using any of the QColor constructor methods

color_border
   Specified using any of the QColor constructor methods

horizontal_anchor_point
   Integer value

name
   Name of the marker (e.g. circle, square, etc)

offset
   Specified as an x,y integer offset

offset_unit
   MM or MapUnit

outline_width
   Integer value

outline_width_unit
   MM or MapUnit

scale_method
   diameter or area

size
   Integer value

size_unit
   MM or MapUnit

vertical_anchor_point
   Integer value

Keywords and values for QgsLineSymbolV2:

capstyle
   'square', 'flat', or 'round'

color

Specified using any of the QColor constructor methods

customdash

Length and spacing of dash, separated by a semi-colon; e.g. 8;4

customdash_unit

MM or MapUnit

joinstyle

'bevel', 'miter', or 'round'

offset

Specified as an x,y integer offset

offset_unit

MM or MapUnit

penstyle

'no', 'solid', 'dash', 'dot', 'dash dot', 'dash dot dot'

use_custom_dash

1 to use the custom dash

width

Integer value

width_unit

MM or MapUnit

Keywords and values for QgsFillSymbolV2:

border_width_unit

MM or MapUnit

color

Specified using any of the QColor constructor methods

color_border

Specified using any of the QColor constructor methods

offset

Specified as an x,y integer offset

offset_unit

MM or MapUnit

style

'solid', 'horizontal', 'vertical', 'cross', 'b_diagonal', 'f_diagonal', 'diagonal_x', 'dense1', 'dense2', 'dense3', 'dense4', 'dense5', 'dense6', 'dense7'

style_border

'no', 'solid', 'dash', 'dot', 'dash dot', 'dash dot dot'

width_border

Integer value

For example, to create a blue circle marker with a size of 8 and outline width of 2 we would use:

```
sym = QgsMarkerSymbolV2.createSimple({
                                      'name':'circle',
                                      'color':'blue',
                                      'size':'8',
                                      'outline_width':'2'
                                    })
renderer = layer.rendererV2()
renderer.setSymbol(sym)
```

We can create a dashed green line of width 4 using:

```
sym = QgsLineSymbolV2.createSimple({
                                     'penstyle':'dash',
                                     'color':'green',
                                     'width':'4',
                                   })
renderer = layer.rendererV2()
renderer.setSymbol(sym)
```

To create a custom red dashed line with length 8 with space of 4:

```
sym = QgsLineSymbolV2.createSimple({
                                     'color':'red',
                                     'customdash':'8;4',
                                     'use_custom_dash':'1',
                                     'width':'2'
```

```
                                                })
        renderer = layer.rendererV2()
        renderer.setSymbol(sym)
```

To create a blue diagonal cross fill:

```
sym = QgsFillSymbolV2.createSimple({
                                'style':'diagonal_x',
                                'color':'blue',
                                })
        renderer = layer.rendererV2()
        renderer.setSymbol(sym)
```

After setting the symbol, we must refresh the map canvas and legend for the changes to be visible.

There are also properties that can be set to create a symbol using an expression that references data defined values. The keywords for each symbol types are as follows:

QgsMarkerSymbolV2:

```
angle_expression
color_border_expression
color_expression
horizontal_anchor_point_expression
name_expression
offset_expression
outline_width_expression
size_expression
vertical_anchor_point_expression
```

QgsLineSymbolV2:

```
color_expression
width_expression
offset_expression
customdash_expression
joinstyle_expression
capstyle_expression
```

QgsFillSymbolV2:

```
color_expression
color_border_expresssion
width_border_expression
```

These expressions are similar to what you would set using the *Data de-fined properties* button on the *Layer properties* dialog. For example, here is how to create a simple marker that uses the MARKER_SIZE field in a layer's attribute table to set the symbol size.

```
sym = QgsMarkerSymbolV2.createSimple({
                              'name':'circle',
                              'color':'blue',
                              'size_expression':'MARKER_SIZE',
                              'outline_width':'1'
                           })
renderer = layer.rendererV2()
renderer.setSymbol(sym)
```

Expressions can include mathematical operations and more complex con-structs, just as you can do using the *Data defined properties* button.

Symbol Layers

In QGIS, a symbol can have multiple layers. This allows you to create interesting symbology, such as a black highway with striping:

This symbol is composed of four separate layers that are overlaid to create the appearance of a striped highway. Let's use the console to take a look at the symbol:

```
>>> lyr = iface.activeLayer()
>>> renderer = lyr.rendererV2()
>>> symbol = renderer.symbol()
>>> symbol.symbolLayerCount()
4
```

Here we confirmed there are four layers in the symbol by using the *sym-bolLayerCount* method once we fetched the symbol from the layer's ren-derer. We can access individual layers of the symbol using the *symbolLayer* method:

```
>>> sym0 = symbol.symbolLayer(0)
>>> sym0
<qgis.core.QgsSimpleLineSymbolLayerV2 object at 0x121ed89e0>
```

Once we have the symbol layer , we can make changes to it. Lets change the dash pattern of the center line of the highway. Obviously we have to have some knowledge about the layout of the symbol layers in order to select the one we want to change. The ordering of the layers are from the bottom up, starting with zero. Our center line is the top layer, so we fetch it using and index of 3:

```
>>> sym3 = symbol.symbolLayer(3)
```

We can get an overview of the symbol by using the *properties* method:

```
>>> sym3.properties()
{u'use_custom_dash': u'1', u'penstyle': u'dash',
u'offset_unit': u'MM', u'color': u'255,255,0,255',
u'customdash': u'3;2', u'customdash_unit': u'MM',
u'joinstyle': u'bevel', u'width': u'0.36',
u'width_unit': u'MM', u'offset': u'0', u'capstyle': u'square'}
```

Here we see or striping layer has a color of 255,255,0,255 (yellow, no transparency), uses a custom dash layout (u'use_custom_dash': u'1'), with a dash/space setting of 3,2 (u'customdash': u'3;2'). We can change any of these properties using the appropriate "set" method (see the *QgsSimpleLineSymbolLayerV2* API documentation).

In this case, want to use the not so obvious *setCustomDashVector* method to change the pattern to length of 10 and space of 5:

```
>>> sym3.setCustomDashVector([10, 5])
```

The result is:

Using the symbol layer methods allow you to customize symbology for layers on your map. If you look at the available methods, you'll notice that we also have access to data defined properties and can tweak them in our code as well.

For working with fill and marker symbol layers, see the API documentation for *QgsSimpleFillSymbolLayerV2* and *QgsSimpleMarkerSymbolLayerV2*.

Using Styles

The QgsMapLayer class provides a number of methods to work with styles, including:

- *saveNamedStyle*
- *loadNamedStyle*
- *saveDefaultStyle*
- *loadDefaultStyle*
- *saveSldStyle*
- *loadSldStyle*

For example, you can symbolize a layer the way you want it, then save the style information to a file:

```
layer = iface.activeLayer()
layer.saveNamedStyle('/tmp/mystyle.qml')
```

Once saved, we can apply the style to a layer:

```
layer.loadNamedStyle('/tmp/mystyle.qml')
iface.mapCanvas().refresh()
iface.legendInterface().refreshLayerSymbology(layer)
```

Note we have to refresh both the canvas and the legend in order to see the applied style. Using the *saveSldStyle/loadSldStyle* methods do the same thing, but save the style as a Styled Layer Descriptor file.

Using *saveDefaultStyle* creates a qml file on disk that will be applied each time the layer is loaded. For example, if we load /gis_data/alaska.shp, style it, and use *saveDefaultStyle*, it creates /gis_data/alaska.qml. The next time we load alaska.shp, the style will be automatically applied.

8.5 Selecting and Working with Features

There are a number of ways to select features from a layer. For example, to iterate through all features, use:

```
for feature in layer.getFeatures():
    # do something with the feature
    print feature.id()
```

The *getFeatures* method actually returns a *QgsFeatureIterator*, allowing us to iterate through all features using the usual Python syntax.

We can access the attributes of a feature using either an index or the name. For the world_borders layer we can get the country name using either of these two methods:

```
name = feature['CNTRY_NAME']
name = feature[2]
```

We can get the index for the CNTRY_NAME field using:

```
idx = feature.fieldNameIndex('cntry_name')
```

Note we can use either upper or lower case and QGIS will recognize the field name.

We can also get features using a rectangle:

```
rectangle = QgsRectangle(-150, 60, -140, 61)
request = QgsFeatureRequest().setFilterRect(rectangle)
for feature in layer.getFeatures(request):
    # do something with each feature
```

To fetch a specific feature by its id, we can use:

```
request = QgsFeatureRequest().setFilterFid(3201)
feature = layer.getFeatures(request).next()
print feature['cntry_name']
```

If we specify a non-existent feature id, an exception will be thrown:

```
request = QgsFeatureRequest().setFilterFid(3201000)
feature = lyr.getFeatures(request).next()
Traceback (most recent call last):
  File "<input>", line 1, in <module>
StopIteration
```

To be safe, you should wrap the request in a try/except block:

```
>>> request = QgsFeatureRequest().setFilterFid(3201000)
>>> try:
...     feature = lyr.getFeatures(request).next()
>>>except StopIteration:
...     print "Feature not found"
Feature not found
```

To select all features in a vector layer use:

```
layer.selectAll()
```

where `layer` is a reference to a valid *QgsVectorLayer*. This selects all the features and highlights them on the map.

To remove the selection use:

```
layer.removeSelection()
```

✐ To work with features in a layer use *getFeatures*. You don't have to also use *selectAll* if you just want to iterate through the features in the layer. Using *selectAll* will create a selection set of all features on the map and highlight them. Care should be taken when selecting features programmatically when a selection set already exists that your code didn't create.

8.6   Editing Attributes

There are a couple of ways to edit attributes:

- Directly through the provider
- Using an edit buffer

Direct editing is easier, but doesn't allow for a rollback of changes. For the next two examples, assume we have a `layer` with the following fields: name and `city`.

If we know the feature id, we can update the name without even entering edit mode:

```
fid = 1
new_name = { 2: 'My New Name'}
layer.dataProvider().changeAttributeValues({fid: new_name})
```

To update the name field, we create a dict (new_name) using the field index as the key, followed by the new name. When we call *changeAttributeValues*, the name field (index of 2) for feature with id of 1 is updated. This requires knowing the field index in advance. We can also get the field index number by first fetching the feature we want to modify:

```
features = layer.getFeatures(QgsFeatureRequest().setFilterFid(1))
feature = features.next()
new_name = { feature.fieldNameIndex('name'): 'My New Name'}
layer.dataProvider().changeAttributeValues({feature.id(): new_name})
```

We can also update multiple attributes and save them using a dict comprehension:

```
1    layer = iface.activeLayer()
2    provider = layer.dataProvider()
3    features = layer.getFeatures(QgsFeatureRequest().setFilterFid(1))
4    feature = features.next()
5    feature['name'] = 'My New Name'
6    feature['city'] = 'Seattle'
7    field_map = provider.fieldNameMap()
8    attrs = {field_map[key]: feature[key] for key in field_map}
9    layer.dataProvider().changeAttributeValues({feature.id(): attrs})
```

See http://loc8.cc/ppg/py_comp for information on list and dict comprehensions.

In *line 3* we get all features with id of 1 and then get the single feature returned in *line 4*. We can then modify the attributes using the syntax shown in *lines 5 and 6*. Rather than manually build up an attribute list, in *line 7* we get the field map from the data provider. This map is just a dict of key, value pairs, where the key is the field name and the value is its index number. In *line 8* we use a dict comprehension to create our attribute dictionary. This gives us a new dict (`attrs`) with the field index number as the key and our feature attributes as the values. We can then use this dict in *line 9* to update the feature.

The advantage here is a simpler syntax for assigning new values and ease in building up the dict needed by *changeAttributeValues*.

Using an edit buffer is best suited to situations where you are providing a custom editing experience via a GUI. This gives the user the chance to rollback or cancel changes. For an example of using an editing buffer, see the PyQGIS Cookbook.

8.7 *Saving Images*

You can save the current map canvas as an image:

```
mc = iface.mapCanvas()
mc.saveAsImage('/tmp/nelchina.png')
```

Of course you can also just do it in a one-liner:

```
iface.mapCanvas().saveAsImage('/tmp/nelchina.png')
```

If we look at the QGIS API documentation for *saveAsImage* we find:

```
void QgsMapCanvas::saveAsImage ( QString  theFileName,
                                 QPixmap  *QPixmap = 0,
                                 QString  theFormat = "PNG"
                               )
```

The second argument allows us to specify an alternate *QPixmap* to use as the source of the image. Specifying None uses the map canvas as the source. The last argument allows us to specify the image format (PNG by default).

If we look at the Qt documentation for QPixmap, we find the following formats are supported for read/write:

- BMP
- JPG
- JPEG
- PNG
- PPM
- XBM
- XPM

To save our map canvas as a JPG we would use:

```
iface.mapCanvas().saveAsImage('/tmp/nelchina.png', None, 'JPG')
```

A world file is also created in the same location as your image. This allows you to later add the image to QGIS as a georeferenced raster.

8.8 *Getting QGIS Paths*

When writing plugins or scripts it is often necessary to get information about the paths QGIS is using. For example, if we are writing a plugin that uses Python templates to create output based on user actions, we need to know the path to our installed plugin. Fortunately the API provides an easy way to get at the information—here are a few examples:

- *QgsApplication.pluginPath()*: location of core plugins
- *QgsApplication.prefixPath()*: location where QGIS is installed
- *QgsApplication.qgisSettingsDirPath()*: location of user settings
- *QgsApplication.iconsPath()*: location of icons used in QGIS

From the console, we can get a summary of the paths used in QGIS using *showSettings*:

```
print QgsApplication.showSettings()
Application state:
QGIS_PREFIX_PATH env var:
Prefix:              /dev1/apps/qgis
Plugin Path:         /dev1/apps/qgis/lib/qgis/plugins
Package Data Path:   /dev1/apps/qgis/share/qgis
Active Theme Name:   default
Active Theme Path:   :/images/themes/default/
Default Theme Path:  :/images/themes/default/
SVG Search Paths:    /dev1/apps/qgis/share/qgis/svg/
    /home/gsherman/.qgis2//svg/
User DB Path: /dev1/apps/qgis/share/qgis/resources/qgis.db
```

These paths are from my development install of QGIS on a Linux box—yours
will be different.

The *showSettings* method is not really useful in a script or plugin since it
returns a string containing line returns and tab characters. It's mainly useful
for debugging and development.

Getting the Path to Your Installed Plugin

Often you need to know where your plugin is installed, so you can access
additional resources such as templates and help files. There is more than
one way to get the path to your plugin, but the surest way is to use *QgsApplication.qgisUserDbFilePath*:

```
>>> QgsApplication.qgisUserDbFilePath()
u'/Users/gsherman/.qgis2//qgis.db'
```

This gives us the path to the `qgis.db` that is created for each user. Earlier
we talked about where plugins are stored and learned, regardless of operating system, the `.qgis2/python/plugins` portion of the path is the same.
Knowing this, we can create the full path to where our plugin is installed
using *os.path.join* and *QFileInfo*:

os.path.join assembles path components in an intelligent, OS compatible way.

```
>>> QFileInfo(QgsApplication.qgisUserDbFilePath()).path()
u'/Users/gsherman/.qgis2/'

>>> plugin_dir = os.path.join(
...     QFileInfo(QgsApplication.qgisUserDbFilePath()).path(),
...     'python/plugins')
>>> plugin_dir
u'/Users/gsherman/.qgis2/python/plugins'
```

To complete the full path, we just add our plugin name:

```
>>> plugin_path = os.path.join(plugin_dir, 'my_plugin')
u'/Users/gsherman/.qgis2/python/plugins/my_plugin'
```

Or, all in one step:

```
>>> plugin_path = os.path.join(
...     QFileInfo(QgsApplication.qgisUserDbFilePath()).path(),
...     'python/plugins/my_plugin')
>>> plugin_path
u'/Users/gsherman/.qgis2/python/plugins/my_plugin'
```

8.9   Messages and Feedback

Feedback from your plugin or script is important, both for you during development and after your work has been deployed. There are a number of ways to provide feedback:

- *QMessageBox*: A Qt class that pops up a message dialog box that the user must take action on
- *QgsMessageLog*: A QGIS class that writes a message to the log message window
- *QgsMessageBar*: A QGIS class that puts a message bar at the top of the map canvas

Let's take a look at each method.

Using QMessageBox

Using a popup message box is a valid way to provide feedback or information. The downside is, it can get in the way of what you're trying to accomplish, particularly when presenting just a bit of information.

We saw an example of QMessageBox in Section 5.4, Static Public Member Functions, on page 55.

QMessageBox is a Qt class, not part of the QGIS API. It is quite flexible and can be used to present information, warnings, and critical messages.

The *QMessageBox* provides three static methods for popping up a message:

- *QMessageBox.information*
- *QMessageBox.warning*
- *QMessageBox.critical*

There are some optional arguments we can supply, however for a simple popup message, the functions are called like this:

```
QMessageBox.information(parent, title, text)
```

The *parent* argument is the GUI element that "owns" the message box. Typically you can specify *None* and it will work fine. To make the box a child of the main QGIS window, you can use *iface.mainwWindow()*:

```
QMessageBox.information(iface.mainwWindow(),
                       'Important Information',
                       'This is an important message')
```

The difference between `information`, `warning`, and `critical` is the icon displayed in the box.

Using QgsMessageLog

QGIS logs messages to a special panel. You can access the message panel from the `View->Panels->Log Messages` menu or by clicking on the yellow triangle icon at the bottom right of the status bar. The messages are organized by tabs that indicate the source of the message.

To log a message to your own custom tab, use something like this:

```
QgsMessageLog.logMessage('SuperZoom plugin intialized and ready',
                         'SuperZoom',
                         QgsMessageLog.INFO)
```

The first argument is the message, the second the tag that will be used as the tab name, and the last is the message level.

You can see from Figure 8.2, on the facing page that entering the above example from the console creates a new tab named *SuperZoom* and writes the message and level to it.

QgsMessageLog isn't well suited to providing user feedback as it may go unnoticed. It is good for logging events, especially during development of scripts and plugins.

Using QgsMessageBar

A nice way to provide user feedback is by using a *QgsMessageBar*:

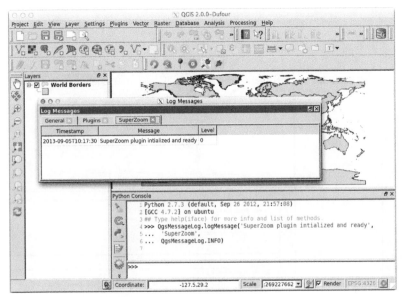

Figure 8.2: Custom Message written to the Log Window

```
iface.messageBar().pushMessage("Title","Message", QgsMessageBar.WARNING, 2)
```

This will place a message bar at the top of the map canvas. The message consists of a title, the message, and a button to dismiss the message. The look of the message is controlled by the level argument and the duration in seconds is specified by the last argument.

Figure 8.3, on the next page shows the result when we enter the following in the console:

```
iface.messageBar().pushMessage("SuperZoom",
                     "You specified an invalid zoom level",
                     QgsMessageBar.CRITICAL,
                     10)
```

The message has a red background, a "critical" icon, and stays on screen for 10 seconds.

If you notice the console commands in Figure 8.3, on the following page, we imported the *QgsMessageBar* class prior to displaying the message bar:

```
from qgis.gui import QgsMessageBar
```

Figure 8.3:   Displaying a Critical
QgsMessageBar

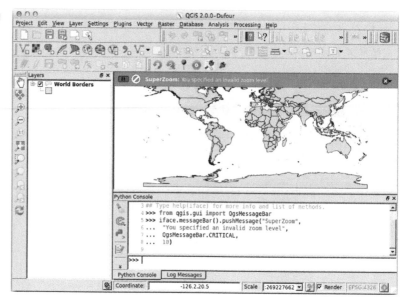

This is because we reference it to specify the level (*QgsMessageBar.CRITICAL*) and by default, the console doesn't import it.

Any time you get a *NameError* when working with the API, it means you need to import the module containing the object you are referencing. This only needs to be done once in a script or console session.

There are actually two implementations of the *pushMessage* method we can use. Looking at the QGIS API documentation for *QgsMessageBar* we find::

```
void QgsMessageBar::pushMessage(const QString & text,
                                QgsMessageBar::MessageLevel level = INFO,
                                int duration = 0
                                )
```

```
void QgsMessageBar::pushMessage(const QString & title,
                                const QString & text,
                                QgsMessageBar::MessageLevel level = INFO,
                                int duration = 0
                                )
```

These are the C++ definitions, but we won't let that bother us. The first implementation supports only a message, whereas the second supports a title and message. Both methods include the level and duration. When you see an equal sign (=) in a method definition it specifies a default value. In the case of *pushMessage*, the level defaults to *INFO* and the duration to 0, meaning the message will remain until the user closes it. You can actually create an *INFO* message using a single argument:

```
iface.messageBar().pushMessage("You specified an invalid zoom level")
```

If you want to provide more context, use the second method:

```
iface.messageBar().pushMessage("SuperZoom",
                              "You specified an invalid zoom level")
```

8.10   Refreshing the Map and Legend

You have probably noticed that changes to symbology or adding/editing features don't affect the map or legend display. We've used both of these methods in previous examples, but here they are again for reference:

```
# refresh the map
iface.mapCanvas().refresh()
# refresh the legend
iface.legendInterface().refreshLayerSymbology(layer)
```

Refreshing the legend requires you to pass a reference to the layer.

8.11   Creating a Map Tool

Often you'll find you need a custom map tool to interact with the map canvas. The simplest example is a tool based on *QgsMapToolEmitPoint*, which emits the coordinates of a mouse click on the canvas.

Suppose we want a tool to create a straight line on the map. We accomplish this by subclassing *QgsMapToolEmitPoint* and adding the methods we want to override. Our tool should take the first click as the start point, draw a rubber band from the first point as the mouse is moved across the canvas. The next click then defines the end point and we can create the line.

To implement these features we need the following methods from the *QgsMap-ToolEmitPoint* base class:

- *canvasPressEvent*
- *canvasMoveEvent*

Here is an implementation of the map tool:

```python
from PyQt4.QtCore import pyqtSignal, Qt
from PyQt4.QtGui import QColor
from qgis.core import QgsGeometry, QgsPoint
from qgis.gui import QgsMapToolEmitPoint, QgsRubberBand


class ConnectTool(QgsMapToolEmitPoint):
    """ Map tool to connect points."""

    line_complete = pyqtSignal(QgsPoint, QgsPoint)
    start_point = None
    end_point = None
    rubberband = None

    def __init__(self, canvas):
        self.canvas = canvas
        QgsMapToolEmitPoint.__init__(self, canvas)

    def canvasMoveEvent(self, event):
        if self.start_point:
            point = self.toMapCoordinates(event.pos())
            if self.rubberband:
                self.rubberband.reset()
            else:
                self.rubberband = QgsRubberBand(self.canvas, False)
                self.rubberband.setColor(QColor(Qt.red))
            # set the geometry for the rubberband
            points = [self.start_point, point]
            self.rubberband.setToGeometry(QgsGeometry.fromPolyline(points),
                                          None)

    def canvasPressEvent(self, e):
        if self.start_point is None:
            self.start_point = self.toMapCoordinates(e.pos())
        else:
            self.end_point = self.toMapCoordinates(e.pos())
            # kill the rubberband
            self.rubberband.reset()
            # line is done, emit a signal
            self.line_complete.emit(self.start_point, self.end_point)
            # reset the points
            self.start_point = None
            self.end_point = None
```

Let's step through the code to see how it works.

First we need some of the usual imports (*lines 1-4*), along with one we haven't seen before: pyqtSignal—more on that in just a bit.

In *line 7* we see the class declaration for *ConnectTool* and note that it subclasses *QgsMapToolEmitPoint*. As we said, this gives us all the functionality of the base class, along with the ability to override it to customize the behavior.

In *line 10* we are declaring a Qt signal named *line_complete*, using the pyqtSignal keyword. We'll emit this signal when our line is complete, passing along the start and end points as *QgsPoint* objects. When using pyqtSignal, you can create a signal either with or without arguments. When specifying arguments, you declare them using their Python types—in our case, *QgsPoint*.

We also declare and set our start, end, and rubberband attributes to None in *lines 11-13*.

Next our *__init__* method (*lines 15-17*) sets things up, including storing a reference to the map canvas (which we must pass to it). You'll notice on *line 17* that we are calling the init method of the parent class. This is important to get things initialized properly.

The next method we need to override is *canvasMoveEvent*, which we do in *lines 19-30*. This event is fired each time the mouse moves on the canvas, providing us with the coordinate information. We can use this to draw a rubberband from the start point to the current cursor position.

We need a starting point for our rubberband; we check for that in *line 20*, and if it exists, we get the click point in *line 21*. Next we check to see if we have a rubberband object in *line 22*. If we do, we reset it (because it is going to change), otherwise we create the rubberband and set its color to red (*lines 24-26*).

To set the rubberband's geometry, we use the start_point and the current location of the mouse cursor, as contained in the event. *Line 28* creates the list needed to set the geometry, which is done in *lines 29 and 30*. This will cause the rubberband to appear on the canvas. As we move the mouse, *canvasMoveEvent* is called repeatedly and the rubberband's geometry is updated, making it appear to move with the cursor.

The last method from our base class that we will override is the *canvasPressEvent* (*lines 32-43*). This event is fired whenever there is a mouse click on the map canvas and we use it to set our start and end points. The event includes information about the location of the click, as well as which button was used and any keyboard modifiers in play. For our purposes, we're only interested in two things: the fact that a mouse button was clicked and the location of the click.

In *line 33* we check to see if we don't yet have a start point and if so, set it in *line 34*. Otherwise, the click is our end point and we set it, reset the rubberband, emit the `line_complete` signal, then clear our start/end points (*lines 35-43*).

Notice that prior to setting either `start_point` or `end_point`, we use the *toMapCoordinates* method to convert from screen to map coordinates (*lines 34 and 36*).

In *line 40* we emit our custom signal. The signal, along the two arguments (start and end points) is emitted and any class or method that has connected to the signal will catch it. The start and end points can then be used to create a new feature or do something else useful.

Using the Map Tool

To use our new map tool we'll create a class that implements the map tool and creates the line based on the two points clicked:

1. Create it:

    ```
    map_tool = ConnectTool(self.canvas)
    ```

2. Create an action to enable it:

    ```
    self.connect_action = QAction(
            QIcon(":/ourapp/connect_icon"),
            "Connect",
            self)
    ```

3. Add the action to our toolbar:

    ```
    self.toolbar.addAction(self.connect_action)
    ```

4. Connect the action to a method that sets the map tool:

```
self.connect_action.triggered.connect(self.connect_pt)
```

5. Create the method that sets the map tool:

```
def connect_pt(self):
    self.map_canvas.setMapTool(self.tool_connect)
```

6. Create the method that creates the new line:

```
def connect_complete(self, pt1, pt2):
    # create the line from the points
    QMessageBox.information(None,
                    "Connect Tool",
                    "Creating line from %s to %s"
                    % (pt1.toString(), pt2.toString()))
```

7. Connect the line_complete signal of the map tool to the connect_complete method to create the line:

```
self.tool_connect.line_complete.connect(self.connect_complete)
```

You'll see this in action in Chapter 12, Writing a Standalone Application, on page 161.

8.12   Adding Existing Tools to a Custom Toolbar

In addition to adding your own tools to a custom toolbar (such as one you create for a plugin), you can add existing QGIS tools as well. This may seem redundant, but if you are creating a plugin that has its own toolbar and makes use of some standard QGIS tools, it makes sense to put them all in one place to improve the user experience.[22]

[22] The cool kids call this *UX*.

For example, let's say we have a toolbar in our plugin class referenced as self.toolbar and our plugin also has stashed the qgis.utils.iface object in self.iface. Here is how we would add the select by rectangle tool to our toolbar in the initialization of the GUI:

```
rect_select = self.iface.actionSelectRectangle()
self.toolbar.addAction(rect_select)
```

That's all there is to it. The action is added to our toolbar and shows up with the same icon as in the QGIS *Manage Layers* toolbar. The tool is ready to use and performs exactly like the original.

8.13   Accessing an Existing Plugin

Sometimes you may want to access the capabilities of an existing plugin from your own script or plugin. While this requires an understanding of the methods and classes in the target plugin, it can be very useful.

PinPoint: http://loc8.cc/ppg/pinpoint

The qgis.utils module provides a data structure we can use to identify which plugins are available and get a reference to one of interest. For this example, we'll use the *PinPoint* plugin that allows you to place a pin with a label at a location on the map. In addition to the usual plugin boilerplate, *PinPoint* has the following methods:

* create_pin_layer()
* place_pin(point, button)

The first method creates a memory layer for the pins and the second method places the pin based on the location of the user click. In order to use the methods of the *PinPoint* plugin, we first need to make sure it is loaded and active. The qgis.utils.plugins dict contains all loaded plugins, keyed by name. We can access *PinPoint* as follows:

```
>>> pp = qgis.utils.plugins['pinpoint']
>>> pp
<pinpoint.pinpoint.PinPoint instance at 0x9efba4c>
```

While this works when *PinPoint* is loaded, we don't fare so well when it's not:

```
pp = qgis.utils.plugins['pinpoint']
Traceback (most recent call last):
  File "<input>", line 1, in <module>
KeyError: 'pinpoint'
```

The answer is to check first before we try to use it:

```
if 'pinpoint' in qgis.utils.plugins:
    pp = qgis.utils.plugins['pinpoint']
    pp
<pinpoint.pinpoint.PinPoint instance at 0x9efba4c>
```

Now that we know how to get a reference to the *PinPoint* plugin, here's the code we would use to create the pin layer and place a pin at coordinate 100, 100:

```
if 'pinpoint' in qgis.utils.plugins:
    pp = qgis.utils.plugins['pinpoint']
    pp.create_pin_layer()
    pp.place_pin(QgsPoint(100,100), 1)
```

The call to place_pin will popup a dialog so we can enter the name for the pin and when we click OK, the pin is placed on our newly created memory layer.

As I mentioned at the start, we need to know something about the code in *PinPoint*, such as the fact that place_pin expects a *QgsPoint* for the location and the button argument takes an integer value. To place additional pins, we only need to call *place_pin*—we wouldn't use *create_pin_layer* again as this would add yet another memory layer to our map canvas.

8.14 Setting Up a Repository

As we said before, it's best to contribute your plugins to the QGIS master repository so they can be shared with others. There are times when you may need an internal repository, specifically during team development or testing.

This isn't a common practice, but useful when developing in a collaborative environment.

Setting up a repository requires a machine with a web server and consists of two steps:

1. Creating an XML file in a web accessible directory that describes the plugin(s) included in the repository

2. Uploading the plugin zip file to a web directory for download by the QGIS Plugin Manager

Here is an example of a simple plugins.xml file:

```
1   <?xml version = '1.0' encoding = 'UTF-8'?>
2   <?xml-stylesheet type='text/xsl' href='/contributed.xsl' ?>
3   <plugins>
4     <pyqgis_plugin name='ScriptRunner' version='1.992'>
5       <description>Run Python scripts </description>
6       <version>1.992</version>
7       <qgis_minimum_version>2.0</qgis_minimum_version>
8       <homepage></homepage>
9       <file_name>scriptrunner.zip</file_name>
10      <author_name>Gary Sherman</author_name>
11      <download_url>http://example.com/qgis_plugins/scriptrunner.zip</download_url>
12      <uploaded_by>gsherman</uploaded_by>
```

```
13        <create_date>2013-07-05</create_date>
14        <update_date>None</update_date>
15        <experimental>False</experimental>
16     </pyqgis_plugin>
17   </plugins>
```

This example defines one plugin: *ScriptRunner*. Each plugin in the repository is defined within a set of *pyqgis_plugin* tags. The requirements are pretty much self-explanatory. In order for QGIS to be able to fetch and install the plugin, the zip file must be correctly specified in the *download_url* tag.

With the `plugins.xml` file created, place it where it can be accessed by HTTP. For example, you could use a URL similar to this, replacing *example.com* with the domain name of your server: *http://www.example.com/plugins.xml.*

Once you have setup the repository, add it to the *Plugin Manager* using the *Settings* tab (see Figure 8.4).

Figure 8.4: Adding a Repository to Plugin Manager

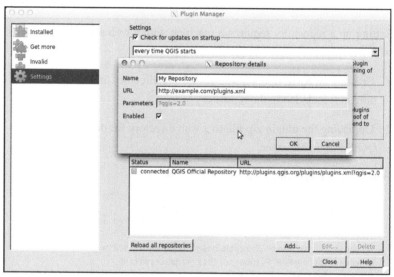

When *Plugin Manager* fetches from the configured repositories, your plugin(s) will show up in the list of available plugins.

Next up, we'll look at extending the API, then move on to writing a plugin.

8.15 Exercises

1. Find the `qgis.utils` module in your QGIS install and open it in a text editor. Examine the methods and data structures available.

2. Create a point memory layer with an `id` and `name` field, add some features to it, and add it to the map canvas.

3. Write a script to turn on labeling for the point layer you created and label each feature using the name field.

4. Using the point layer, write a script that allows you to edit the name for a selected feature by prompting for the new name, then saving it to the attribute table.

9

Extending the API

In our PyQGIS programming efforts, we aren't restricted to using the functionality the API provides—we can extend it by writing our own functions and classes.

In this chapter, we will work up a little "wrapper" script that makes working with layers and colors a bit easier. Our goal here is to simplify the adding of vector and raster layers. In addition, we'll write a function to simplify changing the color of a layer and updating the legend.

9.1   The Imports

To begin with, our wrapper will only support OGR and GDAL layers. For this we will need to import not only the PyQt4 and QGIS modules, but OGR and GDAL as well. Here are the imports we need:

Listing 9.1: wrapper.py: The Imports

```
1  import os
2
3  from PyQt4.QtGui import *
4
5  from qgis.utils import iface
6  from qgis.core import *
7
8  from osgeo import ogr
9  from osgeo import gdal
```

As you look through the listings, think of ways you could refactor the code to make it more concise.

We need the PyQt4.QtGui module because we are going to use the *QColor* class to set the color for our vector layers. We'll also use some classes from the qgis.core and qgis.iface modules. Lastly, the ogr and gdal modules are needed so we can identify what type of layer we are adding—this will become clear in the next couple of code snippets.

9.2   The addLayer Function

Our *addLayer* function takes a URI (in this case a path) and an optional *name* parameter:

Listing 9.2: wrapper.py: addLayer Function

```
12  def addLayer(uri, name=None):
13      """ Generic attempt to add a layer by attempting to
14          open it in various ways"""
15      # try to open using ogr
16      lyr = ogr.Open(uri)
17      if lyr:
18          return addOgrLayer(uri, name)
19      else:
20          # try to open using gdal
21          lyr = gdal.Open(uri)
22          if lyr:
23              return addGdalLayer(uri, name)
24          else:
25              return None
```

In *addLayer* we assume we are getting either a path to an OGR supported vector layer or a GDAL raster. In *line 16* we try to open it using OGR by calling the *ogr.Open* function. If OGR can open it, we know it is a valid vector layer, so we pass the URI and optional name off to the *addOgrLayer* function to add it to the map canvas. If *ogr.Open* returns *None*, we try to open it as a GDAL raster in *line 21*. If this succeeds we add it to QGIS using the *addGdalLayer* function. If neither of these methods are successful, we return None, indicating we couldn't add the layer.

Let's take a look at the *addOgrLayer* and *addGdalLayer* functions to see how they add vector and raster layers to the map.

9.3   The addOgrLayer and addGdalLayer Functions

Here is the code for the two functions that do the real work:

Listing 9.3: wrapper.py: addOgrLayer and addGdalLyer Functions

```
28  def addOgrLayer(layerpath, name=None):
29      """ Add an OGR layer and return a reference to it.
30          If name is not passed, the filename will be used
31          in the legend.
32
33          User should check to see if layer is valid before
34          using it."""
35      if not name:
36          (path, filename) = os.path.split(layerpath)
37          name = filename
38
39      lyr = QgsVectorLayer(layerpath, name, 'ogr')
40      return QgsMapLayerRegistry.instance().addMapLayer(lyr)
41
42
43  def addGdalLayer(layerpath, name=None):
44      """Add a GDAL layer and return a reference to it"""
45      if not name:
46          (path, filename) = os.path.split(layerpath)
47          name = filename
48
49      lyr = QgsRasterLayer(layerpath, name)
50      return QgsMapLayerRegistry.instance().addMapLayer(lyr)
```

By the time *addLayer* calls either *addOgrLayer* or *addGdalLayer*, we know that we have a valid layer. Let's first look at what happens when adding a vector layer.

In *lines 35-37* we check to see if a custom name for the layer was passed. If so we use it, otherwise the filename is used in the legend.

In *line 39* the layer is created by passing the path, name, and the data provider key ('ogr') to *QgsVectorLayer*. In *line 40* we add it to the map using the *addMapLayer* method of the *QgsMapLayerRegistry* class and return a reference to the layer.

Adding a raster works in much the same way in *lines 43-50*, passing the path and name to *QgsRasterLayer*, adding it to the map, and returning a reference to it.

Let's see how we would use what we have so far to add both a vector and raster layer to the map.

9.4   Using the addLayer Function

The first thing we have to do is make sure our wrapper script can be found. This means it must be in the Python path. There are several ways to do this, including:

- Set the PYTHONPATH environment variable to point to the directory where wrapper.py resides
- Dynamically add the path using sys.path.append
- Place wrapper.py in the QGIS python subdirectory

The last method might seem easy, but when you upgrade or uninstall QGIS, your script may be lost.

Reminder: the code is available from http://locatepress.com/files/pyqgis_code.zip.

In our example, we'll use the second method just to illustrate how it's done. We extracted pyqgis_code.zip to our development directory:

/home/gsherman/development/pyqgis_code

Here is the script that allows us to add the world_borders vector layer and the natural_earth raster to our map canvas using wrapper.py:

```
1   import sys
2   sys.path.append('/home/gsherman/development/pyqgis_code')
3   from wrapper import wrapper
4   lyr_vector = wrapper.addLayer('/data/world_borders.shp', 'World Borders')
5   lyr_raster = wrapper.addLayer('/data/HYP_50M_SR_W.tif', 'Natural Earth')
```

In *line 2* we add the directory containing the wrapper module to the Python path by hardcoding it.

Tip: Adding to `sys.path` on the Fly

If you have a script or plugin that needs to import additional modules located in the same directory, you can do so by adding the following statements to your code:

```
import os
import sys
sys.path.append(os.path.dirname(os.path.realpath(__file__)))
```

This adds the directory where your script resides (contained in `__file__`) to the Python path in a fairly portable manner.

We can load our little script in the Console Editor and run it using the *Run script* button. The result can be seen in Figure 9.1. Notice the order in which we executed our statements resulted in the raster being loaded over the vector layer. You should now realize that using *addLayer* is much easier than the step-by-step way of loading a layer.[23]

[23] Well maybe not a lot easier, but certainly lazier.

Figure 9.1: Results of Using wrapper.py

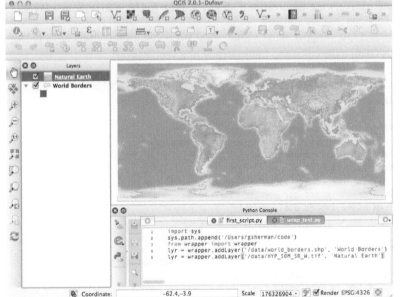

Let's make it easy to remove a layer—in this case we'll use it to remove the natural_earth layer so we can see the world_borders. Here's the function we need to add to wrapper.py:

Listing 9.4: wrapper.py: Remove Layer

```
53  def removeLayer(layer):
54      QgsMapLayerRegistry.instance().removeMapLayer(layer.id())
```

The *removeLayer* function uses the layer's id to remove it from the map. While we can add layers without storing a reference to them, doing so prevents us from working further with them. In our test script we stored references to the vector and raster layers in lyr_vector and lyr_raster respectively.

To remove the natural_earth raster, we use:

```
wrapper.removeLayer(lyr_raster)
```

Running a script from the Console Editor also makes the variables and objects accessible in the console. For example, you can run the script to add vector and raster layers from the editor and then switch to the console and interactively use the wrapper.removeLayer function to remove a layer.

Here's our wrapper script so far—next we'll add a couple functions to help us change the color and transparency of a vector layer:

Listing 9.5: wrapper.py: Using the addLayer Function

```
1   import os
2
3   from PyQt4.QtGui import *
4
5   from qgis.utils import iface
6   from qgis.core import *
7
8   from osgeo import ogr
9   from osgeo import gdal
10
11
12  def addLayer(uri, name=None):
13      """ Generic attempt to add a layer by attempting to
14          open it in various ways"""
15      # try to open using ogr
16      lyr = ogr.Open(uri)
17      if lyr:
```

```
18          return addOgrLayer(uri, name)
19      else:
20          # try to open using gdal
21          lyr = gdal.Open(uri)
22          if lyr:
23              return addGdalLayer(uri, name)
24          else:
25              return None
26
27
28  def addOgrLayer(layerpath, name=None):
29      """ Add an OGR layer and return a reference to it.
30          If name is not passed, the filename will be used
31          in the legend.
32
33          User should check to see if layer is valid before
34          using it."""
35      if not name:
36          (path, filename) = os.path.split(layerpath)
37          name = filename
38
39      lyr = QgsVectorLayer(layerpath, name, 'ogr')
40      return QgsMapLayerRegistry.instance().addMapLayer(lyr)
41
42
43  def addGdalLayer(layerpath, name=None):
44      """Add a GDAL layer and return a reference to it"""
45      if not name:
46          (path, filename) = os.path.split(layerpath)
47          name = filename
48
49      lyr = QgsRasterLayer(layerpath, name)
50      return QgsMapLayerRegistry.instance().addMapLayer(lyr)
51
52
53  def removeLayer(layer):
54      QgsMapLayerRegistry.instance().removeMapLayer(layer.id())
```

9.5 *Changing the Color and Transparency of a Vector Layer*

In order to change the color and transparency, we need a couple of new
functions in our wrapper script. First we'll add one to create a *QColor*
object that contains transparency information:

Listing 9.6: wrapper.py: Changing Color and Transparency

```
57  def createRGBA(color):
58      (red, green, blue, alpha) = color.split(',')
59      return QColor.fromRgb(int(red), int(green), int(blue), int(alpha))
```

The *createRGBA* function accepts a color definition string using four, comma separated integers ranging from 0 to 255 that represent the red, green, blue, and alpha components. It then returns a *QColor* object constructed from each of the components.

For example, to create a red color with 50% transparency, we would use:

```
wrapper.createRGBA('255, 0, 0, 128')
```

Likewise, to create a green color object with no transparency, we would use:

```
wrapper.createRGBA('0, 255, 0, 255')
```

Line 59 creates the color object using *QColor.fromRgb* and returns it.

Now that we can create a custom RGBA color, let's look at the function that actually changes the color of a vector layer on both the map canvas and in the legend:

Listing 9.7: wrapper.py: Changing Colors

```
62  def changeColor(layer, color):
63      """ Change the color of a layer using
64          Qt named colors, RGBA, or hex notation."""
65      if ',' in color:
66          # assume rgba color
67          color = createRGBA(color)
68      else:
69          color = QColor(color)
70
71      renderer = layer.rendererV2()
72      symb = renderer.symbol()
73      symb.setColor(color)
74      layer.setCacheImage(None)
75      iface.mapCanvas().refresh()
76      iface.legendInterface().refreshLayerSymbology(layer)
```

You may remember that we took a look at the ways in which we can create a *QColor* object back in Section 6.4, Exploring Vector Symbology, on page 68. There we saw how to create a *QColor* object using:

- `QColor(Qt.red)`
- `QColor('red')`
- `QColor('#ff0000')`
- `QColor(255,0,0,255)`

Our *changeColor* method in *line 62* accepts any of these parameters for
color. This gives us the widest range of flexibility in creating a custom
color.

In *lines 65-69* we check to see if an RGBA string has been passed in the
color parameter and if so, we create the color using *createRGBA*, otherwise
we create the color directly.

With the color created, we get a reference to the symbol for the layer and
set it in *lines 71-73*.

The last thing to do is refresh the layer and the legend; this is done using
refresh in *line 75* and *refreshLayerSymbology* in *line 76*. Notice also we
invalidated the image cache in *line 74* just in case it exists—this ensures the
repaint will succeed.

Here is the complete listing for wrapper.py:

Listing 9.8: wrapper.py: Complete Script

```
 1  import os
 2
 3  from PyQt4.QtGui import *
 4
 5  from qgis.utils import iface
 6  from qgis.core import *
 7
 8  from osgeo import ogr
 9  from osgeo import gdal
10
11
12  def addLayer(uri, name=None):
13      """ Generic attempt to add a layer by attempting to
14          open it in various ways"""
15      # try to open using ogr
16      lyr = ogr.Open(uri)
17      if lyr:
18          return addOgrLayer(uri, name)
19      else:
20          # try to open using gdal
21          lyr = gdal.Open(uri)
22          if lyr:
23              return addGdalLayer(uri, name)
24          else:
25              return None
26
27
```

```python
28   def addOgrLayer(layerpath, name=None):
29       """ Add an OGR layer and return a reference to it.
30           If name is not passed, the filename will be used
31           in the legend.
32
33           User should check to see if layer is valid before
34           using it."""
35       if not name:
36           (path, filename) = os.path.split(layerpath)
37           name = filename
38
39       lyr = QgsVectorLayer(layerpath, name, 'ogr')
40       return QgsMapLayerRegistry.instance().addMapLayer(lyr)
41
42
43   def addGdalLayer(layerpath, name=None):
44       """"Add a GDAL layer and return a reference to it"""
45       if not name:
46           (path, filename) = os.path.split(layerpath)
47           name = filename
48
49       lyr = QgsRasterLayer(layerpath, name)
50       return QgsMapLayerRegistry.instance().addMapLayer(lyr)
51
52
53   def removeLayer(layer):
54       QgsMapLayerRegistry.instance().removeMapLayer(layer.id())
55
56
57   def createRGBA(color):
58       (red, green, blue, alpha) = color.split(',')
59       return QColor.fromRgb(int(red), int(green), int(blue), int(alpha))
60
61
62   def changeColor(layer, color):
63       """ Change the color of a layer using
64           Qt named colors, RGBA, or hex notation."""
65       if ',' in color:
66           # assume rgba color
67           color = createRGBA(color)
68       else:
69           color = QColor(color)
70
71       renderer = layer.rendererV2()
72       symb = renderer.symbol()
73       symb.setColor(color)
74       layer.setCacheImage(None)
75       iface.mapCanvas().refresh()
76       iface.legendInterface().refreshLayerSymbology(layer)
```

This chapter gives you a simple example of how you can wrap up various QGIS API classes and methods to create new functions. You may have already thought of enhancements that could be implemented in the wrapper. Some suggestions follow in the next section.

9.6   Exercises

1. Identify areas in `wrapper.py` that are potential failure points and add appropriate error checks. For example, what happens if you pass an invalid color specification to *changeColor*?

2. Add a function to reorder the layers in the legend and test it by loading `world_borders.shp`, `natural_earth.tif`, and then switching their order.

3. Add a new function to change the fill style of a vector layer.

4. Similar to the *createRGBA* function, add a new function that accepts four integers and returns a new *QColor* object with transparency.

5. Add a function to add a PostGIS layer using a simple URI.

6. Add a function to add a new memory layer by specifying the fields and CRS in the URI.

10

Writing Plugins

In this chapter we dive into creating a simple plugin from scratch, but first we need to say a few words about the plugin architecture in QGIS.

10.1 Python Plugin Architecture

We covered *where* QGIS stores its plugins in Chapter 4, The QGIS/Python Ecosystem, on page 41; now we want to look in detail at the physical structure of a plugin.

QGIS plugins are packaged in a zip file, consisting of a top-level directory containing the plugin files and any subdirectories. For a minimalistic plugin, a listing of the plugin directory looks like this:

```
|-- testplugin
    |-- __init__.py
    |-- icon.png
    |-- metadata.txt
    |-- resources.qrc
    |-- resources_rc.py
    |-- testplugin.py
    |-- testplugindialog.py
    |-- ui_testplugin.py
    |-- ui_testplugin.ui
```

testplugin
Top-level directory of the plugin.

init.py

This script contains one method (*classFactory*) that initializes the plugin class and makes it known to QGIS.

icon.png

The icon to be used for the plugin when displayed on a QGIS toolbar. The icon should be 24x24 pixels in PNG format.

metadata.txt

The metadata file contains information about the plugin, including the name, description, version, icon, and minimum QGIS version. This file is necessary for QGIS to recognize the plugin.

resources.qrc

Describes resources (e.g. `icon.png`), used by the plugin and its GUI forms.

resources_rc.py

The Python file generated from `resources.py` by the PyQt resource compiler, `pyrcc4`

testplugin.py

The main implementation of your plugin that handles loading, unloading, and execution of the plugin's functions.

testplugindialog.py

The main GUI dialog for the plugin.

ui_testplugin.py

The Python file generated from `ui_testplugin.ui` by the PyQt interface compiler, `pyuic4`.

ui_testplugin.ui

The GUI interface file created by Qt Designer.

We'll look at the details of these plugin components, as well as some additional ones shortly.

Once you have a plugin that works locally, you can package it up in a number of ways. The steps to do it manually are as follows:

1. Create a distribution directory. The name you choose will be the directory name under which the plugin is deployed in QGIS.

2. Copy only the necessary files for your plugin to the distribution directory. If you are using a version control system (VCS) during development, you should do an export to avoid distributing files associated with your VCS.

3. Package the plugin by making a zip archive of it, including the directory

Here is an example of creating a packaged plugin from the command line for an imaginary plugin named super_duper_map:

```
gsherman@ophir:~/development$ ls
super_duper_map
gsherman@ophir:~/development$ mkdir dist
gsherman@ophir:~/development$ cp -r super_duper_map dist
gsherman@ophir:~/development$ cd dist
gsherman@ophir:~/development/dist$ zip -9v super_duper_map.zip super_duper_map/*
  adding: super_duper_map/COPYING (in=18701) (out=7082) (deflated 62%)
  adding: super_duper_map/icon.png       (in=1278) (out=1278) (stored 0%)
  adding: super_duper_map/__init__.py    (in=1460) (out=508) (deflated 65%)
  adding: super_duper_map/resources.py   (in=6402) (out=2556) (deflated 60%)
  adding: super_duper_map/resources.qrc  (in=107) (out=87) (deflated 19%)
  adding: super_duper_map/ui_supermap.py      (in=5049) (out=1328) (deflated 74%)
  adding: super_duper_map/supermapdialog.py   (in=1419) (out=497) (deflated 65%)
  adding: super_duper_map/supermapdialog.pyc  (in=2953) (out=1233) (deflated 58%)
  adding: super_duper_map/supermapdialog.ui   (in=4584) (out=1138) (deflated 75%)
  adding: super_duper_map/supermap.py (in=3550) (out=1282) (deflated 64%)
total bytes=45503, compressed=16989 -> 63% savings
gsherman@ophir:~/development/dist$ ls
super_duper_map  super_duper_map.zip
```

This works on Linux and OS X—adjust the commands accordingly if you are using Windows.

The zip file is now ready for upload to the QGIS repository, but you should probably test it by unzipping into the location of your QGIS plugins to make sure it loads/unloads properly.

Along with the command line, you can use any tool you like to create the archive, including popular zip managers on Windows. The important point is to use zip to package the file and be sure to include the directory in the archive.

10.2   What Happens When You Load a Plugin

This section describes what happens when you load a Python plugin in QGIS. Understanding the basics of the process will help you as you write your own plugins and applications based on the QGIS API.

When QGIS starts up, it examines the contents of your plugin directory to create a list of all valid plugins. Each plugin you have previously enabled is then started by calling the *classFactory* method in *__init__.py*. If the plugin starts successfully, the *initGui* method is called to add entries to the menu and toolbars. The plugin is then added to the list of active plugins.

Any failure during the startup process will result in an exception and an error message will be displayed in QGIS. These errors can be helpful when developing a plugin as they show the file name and line number of the error.

10.3   Creating a Simple Plugin

Let's say we have a need for a plugin that tells us where we are on the map by displaying the coordinates where we click. Our requirements are simple:

A. Click on the map with the mouse

B. Display a dialog box with the X and Y coordinates of the click

Before you protest, it's true we can see the mouse coordinates in the QGIS status bar. We can even tab to the box where they are displayed and copy them but that's not the point—we want to implement it as a plugin to form the basis for a more advance functionality later. We'll start with the Plugin Builder.

Creating a Template with Plugin Builder

Back in the old days (around QGIS version 0.9) we had to create all the boilerplate for a Python plugin by hand. This was tedious and basically the same for each plugin. Fortunately that's no longer the case—we can generate a plugin template using the Plugin Builder.

The Plugin Builder is itself a Python plugin that takes some input from you and creates all the files needed for a new plugin. It's then up to you to customize things and add the code to do something useful. If you did the exercises back in Chapter 4, The QGIS/Python Ecosystem, on page 41, you already have Plugin Builder installed. If not, install it now using the *Plugin Manager* by clicking on the `Plugins->Manage and Install Plugins` menu.

Let's generate the structure for our `Where Am I?` plugin by clicking on the `Plugin Builder` tool or menu item. We are presented with a dialog that contains all the fields needed to create the plugin. On the left side of the plugin dialog you'll see some hints about what is expected for each field.

Figure 10.1, on the next page shows all the fields needed to generate the plugin.

When we click OK, the Plugin Builder generates the files needed for your plugin. In addition to the ones we saw in Section 10.1, Python Plugin Architecture, on page 131, several additional files have been created for us:

Makefile
> This is a GNU makefile that can be used to compile the resource file `resources.qrc` and the user interface file (`.ui`). This requires gmake and works on both Linux and Mac OS X and should also work with the OSGeo4W shell on Windows.

help
> This directory contains the files needed to begin documenting your plugin using Sphinx.

Sphinx is a Python documentation generator available at http://sphinx-doc.org.

i18n
> Empty directory to be used for creating translations of your plugin.

plugin_upload.py
> A Python script to upload the plugin to the QGIS plugin repository. Typically, you would use the web interface at `http://plugins.qgis.org` instead of this script.

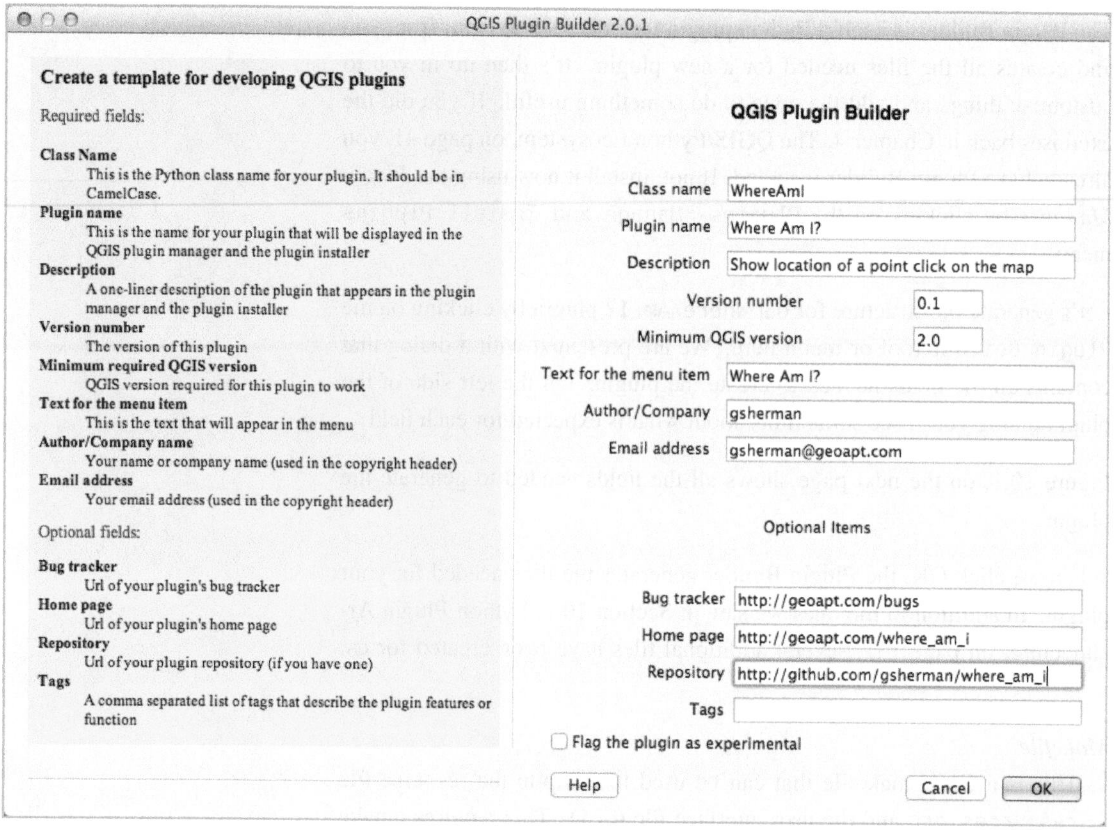

Figure 10.1: Generating a Plugin with
Plugin Builder

README.html and README.txt

The README files contain information about the generated plugin and
the next steps to take in customizing it.

After the plugin generates the needed files, a results dialog is shown that
contains some helpful information, as shown in Figure 10.2, on the next
page.

You'll notice the naming of a number of the files is based on a lower case
version of the name you provide for your plugin, in this case whereami.

The results dialog contains useful information, including:

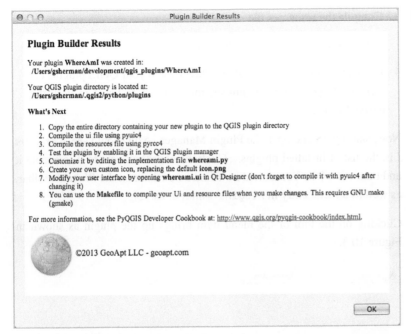

Figure 10.2: Results of Plugin Builder

- Where the generated plugin was saved
- The location of your QGIS plugin directory
- Instructions on how to install the plugin
- Instructions on how to compile the resource and user interface files
- How to customize the plugin to make it do something useful

As we mentioned, this same information can be found in either of the README files in the generated plugin's directory.

Trying the Plugin

Our generated plugin is almost fully functional. The only thing we need to do is compile the resource and user interface files, then place whereami in our plugin directory:

1. Change to the directory where you saved the plugin

2. Compile the ui file

    pyuic4 -o ui_whereami.py ui_whereami.ui

3. Compile the resources file

    pyrcc4 -o resources_rc.py resources.qrc

4. Copy the entire whereami plugin directory to your QGIS plugins directory. If you need a reminder, the location as listed in both the
   README files.

Now, start QGIS and open the Plugin Manager—you should see *Where Am
I* in the list of installed plugins. Click the checkbox next to it to enable it
and then click OK. You should now find a new icon on the *Plugins* toolbar,
as well as a menu entry in Plugins->Where Am I?.

Plugin Manager lists plugins by their
description, not the plugin name.

Clicking on the tool or the menu item brings up the plugin as shown in
Figure 10.3.

Figure 10.3: Running Our New Plugin

It's not much to look at yet, but it is fully functional in the following ways:

- It loads, adding menu and toolbar items
- Running it brings up a dialog window with two buttons
- Clicking OK emits the accept() signal and closes the window
- Clicking Cancel emits the reject() signal and closes the window

We'll talk more about the accept() and reject() signals later on.

Now that we have a working template, we can customize it to do something
useful. First we'll look at how you can customize the icon used for the

plugin, rather and using the default generated by *Plugin Builder*.

We also need to tweak the GUI to add a single box where we will report the coordinates of the map click.

10.4   Customizing the Icon

The icon is just a PNG image that will be used in the toolbar when we activate our plugin. The only real requirement is that it be 24-by-24 pixels so it will fit nicely on the toolbar. You can also use other formats (XPM for one), but PNG is convenient, and there are a lot of existing icons in that format.

By default, the icon created by *Plugin Builder* looks like this:

This is fine for getting started, but you really don't want your plugin using the same icon as dozens of others. You have two options for changing the icon:

- Create a new icon using a graphics program
- Download an existing icon

Of course, you don't have to change the icon during development—the default created by Plugin Builder works fine. For our example, here is a simple "question mark" icon I created using Gimp[24]:   [24] http://gimp.org

Now all we need to do is to modify the resources file to use our new icon.

Modifying the Resources File

First, let's take a look at what's in resources.qrc that *Plugin Builder* created for us:

```
<RCC>
    <qresource prefix="/plugins/whereami" >
        <file>icon.png</file>
    </qresource>
</RCC>
```

This resource file uses a prefix to prevent naming clashes with other plugins. It's good to make sure your prefix will be unique—usually using the name of your plugin is adequate (*Plugin Builder* created the prefix for you based on the plugin name). To add our customized icon, we need to replace the generated file name (icon.png) with our customized icon, which I named whereami.png:

```
<RCC>
    <qresource prefix="/plugins/whereami" >
        <file>whereami.png</file>
    </qresource>
</RCC>
```

Since we are using a new file name for our icon, we need to make a couple of changes in our code, specifically in metadata.txt and whereami.py.

In metadata.txt we find the icon=icon.png line and change it to match our new icon name:

```
icon=whereami.png
```

In whereami.py, the icon is loaded from the graphic file specified in *line 4*:

```
1    def initGui(self):
2    # Create action that will start plugin configuration
3    self.action = QAction(
4        QIcon(":/plugins/whereami/icon.png"),
5        u"Where Am I?", self.iface.mainWindow())
6        ...
```

Changing *line 4* to:

```
QIcon(":/plugins/whereami/whereami.png"),
```

will cause the plugin to load our new icon.

With the changes complete and the resource file saved, we need to compile it in order for it to be used by our new plugin:

```
pyrcc4 -o resources.py resources.qrc
```

The -o switch is used to define the output file. If you don't include it, the output of pyrcc4 will be written to the terminal. Now that we have the resources compiled, we need to build the GUI to display the map coordinates when we click on a point.

If you choose to use the default icon created by Plugin Builder you don't have to modify the resources file, but you do have to compile it.

10.5   Customizing the GUI

Looking back at Figure 10.3, on page 138, we can see that the dialog created by *Plugin Builder* is much too big and it lacks a means to display the results of a map click. To shrink it down and make it do something useful, we need to modify the user interface file (`.ui`) and the implementation file (`whereami.py`).

To fix up our GUI, we'll use the same tool that the QGIS C++ developers use: Qt Designer. This is a visual design tool that allows you to create dialog boxes and main windows by dragging and dropping widgets and defining their properties. `Designer` is normally installed along with Qt, so it should be already available on your machine.[25]

Designer is now part of Qt Creator. See `http://loc8.cc/ppg/ qtcreator`.

[25] On some Linux distributions you may have to install additional packages using your package manager.

Let's take a look at what it takes to polish up our GUI for *WhereAmI*. This will be a quick tour—we won't go into all the intricacies of `Designer`. If you want to get into the nitty-gritty, see the excellent documentation for `Designer` on the Qt website and in your Qt documentation directory.

Our GUI is pretty simple; it requires the following components:

- A label describing the results
- A text box containing the X and Y coordinates of the point where we clicked
- A button to close the dialog

To begin, we open our generated dialog box in `Designer` using the `File` menu and selecting `ui_whereami.ui`.

In Figure 10.4, on the following page, you can see the dialog box as generated by *Plugin Builder* in `Designer`, along with the widget palette and the property editor.

Here are the steps we need to modify the GUI:

1. Delete the Close/OK button group by clicking on it and pressing delete

2. Drag and drop a Label widget (found under Display Widgets) to the dialog box

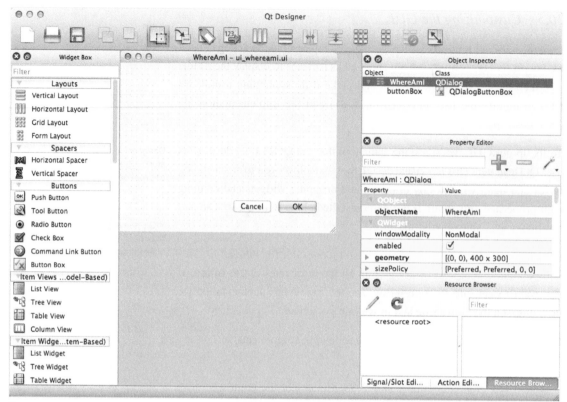

Figure 10.4: The WhereAmI Plugin
GUI in Qt Designer

3. Change the label to read: "Coordinates of map click:"

4. Drag and drop a Line Edit widget (found under Input Widgets) under
    the label and resize it to near the width of the dialog box

5. Drag and drop a Push Button widget (found under Buttons) on the
    dialog box just under the Line Edit widget

6. Double click the newly added button and rename it "Close"

7. Resize the dialog box to eliminate unused space

Our dialog is complete with one exception—the Close button is not hooked
up to do anything when clicked. By default, the Close/OK button group is
wired up to manage accepting (OK) and rejecting (Close) the dialog. We

could have used the button group by deleting just the OK button, however to illustrate wiring up a button to a method we'll do it by hand.

To make our new Close button work, we use the Signal/Slot editor in `Designer`:

1. Click on `Edit->Edit Signals/Slots` in the menu

2. Click and hold on the Close button, then drag the mouse cursor to the empty space on the dialog box and release the mouse to bring up the Configure Connection box

3. On the left panel, click *pressed()*

4. On the right panel, click *reject()*

5. Click OK to make the connection

6. Save the changes using `File->Save` on the menu

Figure 10.5, on the next page shows the connection made between the button's `pressed` signal and the dialog's `reject` slot. This means that, when the button is pressed, the dialog receives the signal and directs it to the reject slot (which is really just a method), and closes the dialog.

You don't need to know the details of how the signal/slot mechanism in Qt works to create simple dialogs like the one for the WhereAmI plugin. As you develop more sophisticated PyQGIS plugins or applications, you will want to delve into it a bit more. We will be making connections manually when we add some code to the WhereAmI plugin.

Once we have all the controls on the form, we're ready to generate some code from it. To convert our completed dialog box to Python, we use the PyQt `pyuic4` command to compile it:

```
pyuic4 -o ui_whereami.py ui_whereami.ui
```

This gives us `ui_whereami.py` containing the code necessary to create the dialog box when the plugin is launched. It's important to maintain the naming convention as the generated Python code relies on specific names in order to find the components it needs. For example, the Python script that

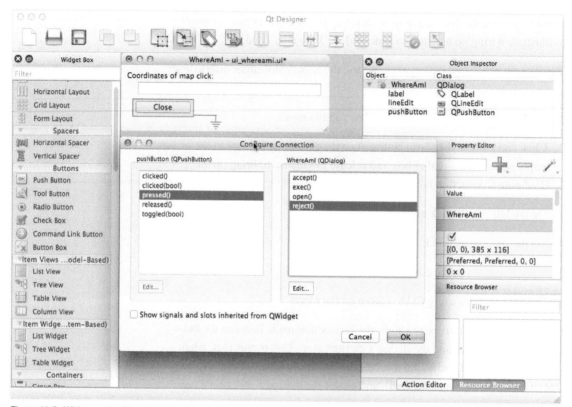

Figure 10.5: Wiring up the Close button to close the Dialog Box when Pressed

initializes the dialog imports `ui_whereami.py`:

```
from ui_whereami import Ui_WhereAmI
```

If the compiled dialog is not named properly the plugin will fail to initialize.

Our GUI is now ready for use.

10.6 Writing the Plugin Code

Now that our GUI and resources are complete, it's time to write some code to get the plugin to do something useful, namely, tell us where we are when we click on the map canvas.

First let's look at the code generated for us by *Plugin Builder*, starting

with the imports and the *__init__* method in the main Python source file,
`whereami.py`:

Listing 10.1: whereami.py: Imports and Init Method

```python
 1   from PyQt4.QtCore import *
 2   from PyQt4.QtGui import *
 3   from qgis.core import *
 4   # Initialize Qt resources from file resources.py
 5   import resources_rc
 6   # Import the code for the dialog
 7   from whereamidialog import WhereAmIDialog
 8
 9
10   class WhereAmI:
11
12       def __init__(self, iface):
13           # Save reference to the QGIS interface
14           self.iface = iface
15           # Create the dialog and keep reference
16           self.dlg = WhereAmIDialog()
17           # initialize plugin directory
18           self.plugin_dir = os.path.join(
19               QFileInfo(QgsApplication.qgisUserDbFilePath()).path(),
20               "/python/plugins/whereami")
```

In *lines 1-3*, we import the PyQt libraries and the QGIS *core* library. *Line 5*
imports our resources file and in *line 7*, the code needed to load and initialize
our GUI dialog is imported. This code is all generated by *Plugin Builder*.
If you need additional Python modules for your plugin, you'll add them in
this section of code—for WhereAmI we don't need anything further.

Line 10 starts the class definition of WhereAmI, the *__init__* method being
defined first. You'll see some of housekeeping items are taken care of in
lines 13-20. Again, we don't need to change anything in these lines of
code. We do however, have to add some additional code to make our plugin
work with the map canvas.

Since WhereAmI depends on a click on the map canvas to do its work, we
must set it up as a *map tool*. This means that when our icon on the toolbar is
clicked, WhereAmI becomes the active map tool in QGIS and is responsible
for handling all clicks on the canvas. It remains active until another map tool
(such as a zoom tool) is selected.

The first step is to create the map tool using the *QgsMapToolEmitPoint* class from the QGIS API. This class implements a map tool that, when clicked, emits a point containing the map coordinates. To create the tool and store it as an attribute of the WhereAmI class we need to import it by adding a new statement to our imports:

```
from qgis.gui import QgsMapToolEmitPoint
```

We also need to add a few lines of code to the *__init__* method:

```
# Store reference to the map canvas
self.canvas = self.iface.mapCanvas()

# Create the map tool using the canvas reference
self.pointTool = QgsMapToolEmitPoint(self.canvas)
```

With these changes, the first section of our code now looks like this, with additions at *line 5* and *lines 24-27*:

Listing 10.2: whereami.py: Adding the Map Tool

```
1   # Import the PyQt and QGIS libraries
2   from PyQt4.QtCore import *
3   from PyQt4.QtGui import *
4   from qgis.core import *
5   from qgis.gui import QgsMapToolEmitPoint
6   # Initialize Qt resources from file resources.py
7   import resources_rc
8   # Import the code for the dialog
9   from whereamidialog import WhereAmIDialog
10
11
12  class WhereAmI:
13
14      def __init__(self, iface):
15          # Save reference to the QGIS interface
16          self.iface = iface
17          # Create the dialog and keep reference
18          self.dlg = WhereAmIDialog()
19          # initialize plugin directory
20          self.plugin_dir = os.path.join(
21              QFileInfo(QgsApplication.qgisUserDbFilePath()).path(),
22              "/python/plugins/whereami")
23
24          # Store reference to the map canvas
25          self.canvas = self.iface.mapCanvas()
26          # Create the map tool using the canvas reference
27          self.pointTool = QgsMapToolEmitPoint(self.canvas)
```

In *line 25* we store a reference to the map canvas. We could just call *self.iface.mapCanvas()* each time we need it, but this saves a few keystrokes for those of us that are lazy programmers.[26]

[26] Laziness is one of the three virtues of a programmer, the other two being impatience and hubris (*Programming Perl*, second edition by Larry Wall, Tom Christiansen, and Randel L. Schwartz, 1996).

In *line 27*, we create the map tool and set its parent to `self.canvas`.

Next, in the *initGui* method, we need to connect a click on the map canvas using our point tool to the method we want to process the information (this can be added anywhere in *initGui*). As of PyQt 4.8, there are two ways to do this:

- The "old" way using *QObject.connect*
- The "new" way using the *connect* method that is available for any object that emits a signal

Let's look at using the old method to connect a click (the *canvasClicked* signal) of our tool to our display method:

```
# connect signal that the canvas was clicked
result = QObject.connect(self.pointTool,
    SIGNAL("canvasClicked(const QgsPoint &, Qt::MouseButton)"),
    self.display_point)
```

Using the old method requires us to know how to write the arguments in the proper form. The new method is much simpler and we'll use it:

```
# connect signal that the canvas was clicked
self.pointTool.canvasClicked.connect(self.display_point)
```

Now when the WhereAmI tool is selected and the map canvas is clicked, the framework will capture the click and the coordinates (as a *QgsPoint* object), and pass control off to our as yet unwritten *display_point* method.

We'll go back and put this all together shortly, but let's look at the *display_point* method first:

Listing 10.3: whereami.py: display_point Method

```
1  def display_point(self, point, button):
2      # report map coordinates from a canvas click
3      self.dlg.hide()
4      coords = "{}, {}".format(point.x(), point.y())
5      self.dlg.ui.lineEdit.setText(str(coords))
6      self.dlg.show()
```

In *line 1* we define the *display_point* method with arguments passed by the signal from the map canvas. If we look up the *canvasClicked* method of *QgsMapToolEmitPoint* in the QGIS API documentation we find this explanation:

```
void QgsMapToolEmitPoint::canvasClicked ( const QgsPoint &  point,
                                          Qt::MouseButton   button )
```

This tells us that our *display_point* method receives a *QgsPoint* object containing the coordinates of the map click, and a button value indicating which button was pushed. Knowing which mouse button was pressed allows us to perform different actions based on how you click on the map. In our simple plugin, we don't care how the click is generated—we just want to display the coordinates.

In *line 3* we hide the dialog so when we show it again it will pop up on top of the main window, otherwise subsequent clicks would result in our dialog always being hidden.

Line 4 creates a string using a format specification and the X and Y values from the *QgsPoint* object using the *x()* and *y()* methods. This results in a formatted string with lots of decimal places:

```
-152.661636888, 65.6374837099
```

As of Plugin Builder 2.0.3, the generated dialog class inherits from both QDialog and the UI class. To refer to any GUI element, you now use self.dlg.elementName rather than self.dlg.ui.elementName.

Line 5 sets the value of the line edit box in our dialog to our formatted result string. To refer to any GUI element we prefix the name with self.dlg.ui. For example, to refer to the label, we would use self.dlg.ui.label. If you're wondering how we know it's *label*, the names of all GUI elements on the dialog can be viewed in the Object Inspector in Designer, as seen in Figure 10.5, on page 144.

Line 6 calls the dialog's *show* method, making it visible.

10.7   One Last Tweak

When using our plugin you may notice that the result dialog pops up in the same place every time, even if we have moved it to a more pleasing location. This can be annoying so we'll make a small change to our code to restore its window position each time it is opened.

When a Qt widget is moved, it generates an event: *QMoveEvent*. We can override this event in our dialog code to store the location of the dialog and pop it up where we want each time.

This involves changes to our dialog code (`whereamidialog.py`) and our plugin (`whereami.py`).

First let's look at the dialog code needed to implement the change:

Listing 10.4: whereamidialog.py

```
1  from PyQt4 import QtCore, QtGui
2  from ui_whereami import Ui_WhereAmI
3  # create the dialog for zoom to point
4
5
6  class WhereAmIDialog(QtGui.QDialog):
7      def __init__(self):
8          QtGui.QDialog.__init__(self)
9          # Set up the user interface from Designer.
10         self.ui = Ui_WhereAmI()
11         self.ui.setupUi(self)
12         # attribute for storing the position of the dialog
13         self.userPos = None
14
15     def moveEvent(self, event):
16         self.userPos = event.pos()
```

We added *line 13* to initialize an attribute that will store the position of the result dialog, setting it to None, the Python way of expressing "absence of value." In other words, we haven't set self.userPos to anything yet—that happens in the moveEvent method on *lines 15 and 16*.

By defining a moveEvent method in our dialog, the PyQt framework will call it instead of the default handler. We receive the event, which is a type of *QMoveEvent*[27], and set the userPos attribute to store the current position of the dialog by calling the *pos()* method of the move event. Every time you move the dialog, the current position is updated.

[27] QMoveEvent: `http://loc8.cc/ppg/qme`

Now we have to make a few changes in the *display_point* method of our main implementation file:

Listing 10.5: whereami.py: Modified display_point Method

```
1      def display_point(self, point, button):
```

```
2          # report map coordinates from a canvas click
3          self.dlg.hide()
4          coords = "{}, {}".format(point.x(), point.y())
5          self.dlg.ui.lineEdit.setText(str(coords))
6          # show the dialog
7          if self.dlg.userPos is not None:
8              self.dlg.move(self.dlg.userPos)
9          self.dlg.show()
```

In *lines 7 and 8* we check to see if the user position has been set and, if so, move the dialog before showing it.

If you try the plugin, you'll notice that you can move the dialog to a convenient position after the first use and it will stay there with all subsequent uses during your QGIS session. Since we didn't write any code to persist the settings, when you exit QGIS, the dialog position is lost.

Figure 10.6 shows the result of using the WhereAmI plugin. Note the results in the plugin match those displayed in the coordinate box of the QGIS status bar.

Figure 10.6: The WhereAmI Plugin in Action

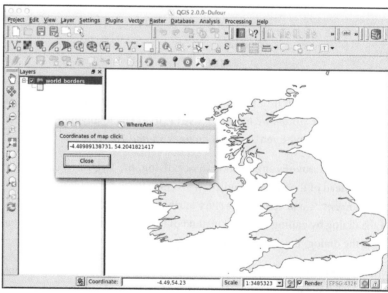

A full listing of `whereami.py` and `whereamidialog.py` can be found in Appendix B: Code Listings, on page 183.

Now that we've written a simple plugin, in the next chapter we'll talk a bit about developing an efficient development workflow.

10.8   Exercises

1. Format the results of the WhereAmI plugin so only three decimal places are shown.

2. Modify the WhereAmI plugin to use a Label widget for displaying coordinates rather than a Line Edit widget.

3. Add a button to the right of the Label or Line Edit widget that copies the results to the clipboard when clicked (hint: see the *QClipboard* class in the Qt documentation).

4. Add a layout to the plugin dialog box so when it is resized, the widgets resize appropriately (hint: use the layout tools in Designer).

5. Using *QSettings* and the *closeEvent* of the dialog, save the dialog position and restore it each time the plugin is loaded.

11

Creating a Development Workflow

Now that we have developed a simple plugin, let's talk a bit about the development process and how to establish a workflow that suits you best.

Software development is an iterative cycle:

Figure 11.1: The Developer's Spiral

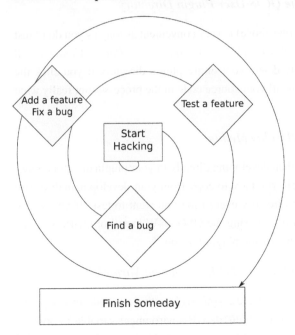

When creating a plugin, we have to deploy it to a location where QGIS can find it in order to test it. Let's examine the options for setting up a workflow.

11.1 Choosing a Development Methodology

We have a number of options:

1. Copy or move the plugin files to your QGIS plugin directory and develop from there.

2. Work within a source code directory (for example, that created by Plugin Builder) separate from your QGIS plugin directory

3. Same as option 2, but use the QGIS_PLUGINPATH environment variable

4. Setup a repository and push your plugin to it for testing

5. Use git to commit your changes then pull to your QGIS plugin directory each time you want to test

Developing from the QGIS User Plugin Directory

This method (option one above) is very convenient as long as you don't test the uninstall feature of your plugin. If you do, the *Plugin Manager* will warn you, yet happily delete your entire plugin directory if you click the Yes button, destroying all your source code in the process—not really what we want.

Using the Develop/Deploy Method

This method is safer than developing directly in your plugin directory, however to test your plugin you have to copy from your development directory to your QGIS plugin directory every time you want to test. If you are on a Unix based system or are using the OSGeo4W install of QGIS, you can create a Makefile to deploy the plugin for you.[28]

[28] Plugin Builder creates a Makefile you can customize for building and deploying your plugin.

Using the QGIS_PLUGINPATH Environment Variable

With this method (option three), you work with your code in a separate directory but use the QGIS_PLUGINPATH environment variable to point to your development directory. When present, QGIS_PLUGINPATH tells QGIS to search additional directories for plugins. Going this route allows you to develop in the directory created by Plugin Builder and test your plugin without any copying or pulling. It is still possible to uninstall your plugin (and destroy your source code) using Plugin Manager if you miss and accidentally click the Yes button.

Using the Repository Method

This method (option four) can be useful but requires a bit of work upfront. You setup a plugin repository (see Section 8.14, Setting Up a Repository, on page 115), then deploy your plugin to it. You can then install onto any machine for testing. I use this method when testing the cross-platform compatibility of a plugin, usually during the latter stages of development.

Using git

The last option in our list of suggested methodologies is to use git to pull changes into your QGIS plugin directory. The steps to use this method are roughly:

1. Create your plugin in any source directory you desire (preferably using Plugin Builder)

2. Change to the directory and initialize a git repository:

    ```
    git init .
    ```

3. Add your source files using git add

4. Develop your plugin and commit the changes using git commit

5. Change to your QGIS plugin directory (see Section 4.6, Python Plugin Specifics, on page 46)

6. Clone your source repository that contains the plugin. For example, if your source code is in /home/myname/myplugin:

    ```
    git clone /home/myname/myplugin
    ```

7. Test the plugin in QGIS

8. Make more edits in the source directory and commit, then change to

the QGIS plugin directory created in step 6 and do `git pull`

9. Test in QGIS and repeat

Regardless of which method you use for development, keeping your source code under version control and pushed to an off-site repository (such as Github or BitBucket) is a good idea.

The Preferred Methodology

So which method should you use? This of course is a matter of opinion, but here is one alternative; a workflow which combines a few of the options we discussed above:

1. Use Plugin Builder to start your plugin, saving it in a directory where you will keep the source code for all your plugins

2. Change to your source directory and put it under source control:

   ```
   git init .
   git add *
   git commit -am 'Initial commit of my great plugin'
   ```

3. Configure the `Makefile` that was generated by Plugin Builder so it can deploy to your QGIS plugin directory

4. Use `make deploy` when ready to test your plugin

5. Use git to push your changes to a remote repository (e.g. Github) on a regular basis

The *Plugin Reloader* plugin can be very useful when developing your plugin. It allows you to reload your plugin after changes are made without having to restart QGIS.

Compiling UI and Resource Files on Windows

If the Makefile generated by Plugin Builder doesn't work on your Windows platform, you can use the following Python script to build your UI and resource files:

Listing 11.1: compile.py

```
# Build QGIS plugin ui and resource files in the current directory
```

```
# Use: python compile.py
# Must be run from the OSGeo4W shell

import glob
import os
import subprocess

ui_files = glob.glob('*.ui')
for ui in ui_files:
    (name, ext) = os.path.splitext(ui)
    print "pyuic4 -o {}.py {}".format(name, ui)
    subprocess.call(["pyuic4.bat", "-o", "{}.py".format(name), ui])

rc_files = glob.glob('*.qrc')
for rc in rc_files:
    (name, ext) = os.path.splitext(rc)
    print "pyrcc4.exe -o {}_rc.py {}".format(name, rc)
    subprocess.call(["pyrcc4.exe", "-o", "{}_rc.py".format(name), rc])
```

✎ You must run the script from the OSGeo4W shell.

11.2 Debugging

When log messages and print statements aren't enough to troubleshoot your
PyQGIS code, you may have to resort to interactive debugging. There are a
several options for debugging your code:

1. The pdb debugger used from the command prompt

2. Remote debugging from your IDE

3. Standalone remote debugger

Using pdb

Using pdb requires us to import the module in our code:

```
import pdb
```

When you want to cause your code to stop and drop into the debugger, place
these lines at the desired breakpoint:

```
pyqtRemoveInputHook()
pdb.set_trace()
```

The key to using pdb is to start QGIS from a terminal. On Linux, you simply run qgis from the command line.

On Mac OS X, you need to use the open command. Assuming QGIS is installed in Applications:

```
open /Applications/QGIS.app/Contents/MacOS/QGIS
```

The Windows version of QGIS doesn't allow us to start it in a way that pdb can attach to the process—you'll have to use one of the other methods listed below.

Once pdb is active in your terminal, you can use commands to list the source, set breakpoints, view the contents of variables, and step through your code. Typing *help* gives you a summary of the available commands, many of which have one letter abbreviations:

```
(Pdb) help

Documented commands (type help <topic>):
========================================
EOF     bt         cont      enable  jump  pp       run      unt
a       c          continue  exit    l     q        s        until
alias   cl         d         h       list  quit     step     up
args    clear      debug     help    n     r        tbreak   w
b       commands   disable   ignore  next  restart  u        whatis
break   condition  down      j       p     return   unalias  where

Miscellaneous help topics:
==========================
exec   pdb

Undocumented commands:
======================
retval  rv
```

For more information and details on using pdb, see the documentation at:

```
http://loc8.cc/ppg/pdb
```

Remote Debugging from an IDE

There are a number of IDEs that support remote debugging, meaning they can attach to a running QGIS project and provide debug capability. Here are two that are known to work with QGIS:

- PyDev (Eclipse)
- PyCharm (commercial)

We talked about installing PyDev in Section 3.2, Using an IDE, on page 37.
For a complete description on configuring and using PyDev to debug a
QGIS plugin, see:

> http://linfiniti.com/2011/12/remote-debugging-qgis-python-plugins-with-pydev/

This blog post contains a complete example starting with creating a simple
plugin to creating the PyDev project and using the remote debugger.

While PyCharm has released a Community Edition at version 3, it does
not support remote debugging. If you want to use PyCharm, you'll need
the Professional Edition. If you choose to go this route, a comprehensive
HowTo for debugging QGIS plugins is available at:

> http://linfiniti.com/2012/09/remote-debugging-qgis-plugins-using-pycharm/

Remote Debugging with Winpdb

If you don't use an IDE or yours doesn't support remote debugging you
can use Winpdb.[29] Despite its name, Winpdb is a cross platform debugging
tool that works on Linux, Mac OS X, and Windows. It does require the
installation of wxPython which is available for each of the three operating
systems.[30]

[29] http://winpdb.org
[30] http://www.wxpython.org

As with pdb, we need to add a few lines of code to enable debugging:

```
import rpdb2
rpdb2.start_embedded_debugger(password)
```

When your code encounters the *start_embedded_debugger* statement, it
will pause and wait five minutes for a debugger to attach. From Winpdb
you then attach to the process using the same password specified in your
code. From that point on you have access to the code within the debugger
as seen in Figure 11.2, on the following page, where our WhereAmI plugin
is being debugged.

We can use the tools to step through the code, examine variables, and set
additional breakpoints.

Figure 11.2: Debugging the Where-
AmI Plugin with Winpdb

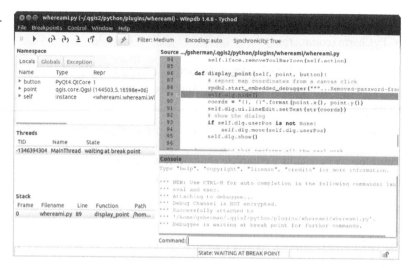

In summary, using a visual debugger (either standalone or part of an IDE)
can be a very efficient way to troubleshoot your code. Being able to attach
to QGIS and test your plugin under actual use is extremely useful.

12

Writing a Standalone Application

Using Qt and the QGIS API, you can create your own standalone GIS application that contains only the functionality you need. Some reasons to do this include:

- You need a custom, streamlined data collection application for field use
- You want to restrict functionality to provide a simple or secure application
- You want to include QGIS functionality in a larger application that isn't necessarily GIS-centric

The main challenge in creating a standalone application is in deployment. If you are targeting a single operating system it is a bit simpler. Before we worry too much about deployment, let's look at creating a simple application that includes a few map tools and a map canvas.

12.1 Designing the Application

First and foremost, a QGIS application is a Qt application—we use the PyQt framework for the GUI.

There are a couple of options for creating the GUI:

1. Use Qt Designer to layout the main window and other GUI elements

2. Create the entire interface in our Python code

We'll use the second method, as it will help you understand more about what's going on "under the hood".

Using PyQt Interactively

Just as you can use the interactive shell to experiment with Python basics, you can also use it to bring up a simple Qt application. Here is a short example that we can try from the Python shell—we'll use this as a starting point on which to build our application.

Listing 12.1: interactive.py

```
1   from PyQt4 import QtGui
2
3   app = QtGui.QApplication([])
4   main_win = QtGui.QMainWindow()
5   frame = QtGui.QFrame(main_win)
6   main_win.setCentralWidget(frame)
7   grid_layout = QtGui.QGridLayout(frame)
8
9   text_editor = QtGui.QTextEdit()
10  text_editor.setText("This is a simple PyQt app that includes "
11                      "a main window, a grid layout, and a text "
12                      "editor widget.\n\n"
13                      "It is constructed entirely from code.")
14  grid_layout.addWidget(text_editor)
15  main_win.show()
16  # Need the following statement if running as a script
17  app.exec_()
```

If you enter these statements (or run them from a script) from the Python shell, you'll get a simple application shown in Figure 12.1, on the next page.

Let's take a quick look at what's going on in the code. In *line 1* we import the *PyQt4.QtGui* module since it contains the classes we need to create our little application. Here's an annotated list of *lines 3-7*:

Line 3: Create the application using the QApplication class

Line 4: Create the main window for our application

Line 5: Create a frame that we will add other widgets to

Line 6: Set the frame as the central widget of our main window (every main window has one)

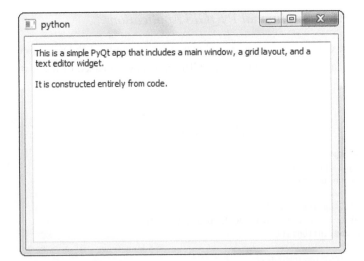

Figure 12.1: A Simple PyQt Application

Line 7: Create a grid layout that has the frame as its parent

These statements setup the basics of our application and window. The grid layout will allow us to have PyQt dynamically resize all our child widgets when the main window is resized.

Now we are ready to add the core of our application; a text edit control in *line 9*. Notice we create it without specifying a parent widget (if it had a parent, it would have been specified as an argument to QtGui.QTextEdit()).

In *lines 10-13* we add some text to our editor, just so we can make sure it's working when we run the app. In *line 14* we add our text editor to the grid layout widget, which will handle the dynamic layout for us.

The last two things are to show the main window in *line 15* and then add *line 17* in case we want to run this code as a script from the command line.

That's a complete GUI app in just seventeen lines of code, although it is not what we would call feature-rich. The fact that you can construct an app and in general use PyQt from the Python shell is a great help in prototyping and learning the API. Let's move our simple code forward and turn it into something spatial.

12.2   Creating a Minimal PyQGIS Application

To begin, we can turn our simple application into a minimal PyQGIS app
that displays a shapefile by adding a QGIS map canvas instead of the text
editor control:

Listing 12.2: interactive_qgis.py

```
1  from PyQt4 import QtGui
2  from qgis.gui import *
3  from qgis.core import *
4
5  app = QtGui.QApplication([])
6  QgsApplication.setPrefixPath("/dev1/apps/qgis", True)
7  QgsApplication.initQgis()
8
9  main_win = QtGui.QMainWindow()
10  frame = QtGui.QFrame(main_win)
11  main_win.setCentralWidget(frame)
12  grid_layout = QtGui.QGridLayout(frame)
13
14  map_canvas = QgsMapCanvas()
15  grid_layout.addWidget(map_canvas)
16  map_canvas.setCanvasColor(QtGui.QColor(255, 255, 255))
17  layer = QgsVectorLayer(
18      '/dev1/gis_data/qgis_sample_data/shapefiles/alaska.shp',
19      'alaska',
20      'ogr')
21  QgsMapLayerRegistry.instance().addMapLayer(layer)
22  canvas_layer = QgsMapCanvasLayer(layer)
23  map_canvas.setLayerSet([canvas_layer])
24  map_canvas.zoomToFullExtent()
25
26  main_win.show()
27
28  # Need the following statement if running as a script
29  app.exec_()
```

This gives us the little application shown in Figure 12.2, on the facing page.
It isn't much to look at—no toolbars, menus, map controls, or legend, just a
map canvas with a single layer. Let's take a deeper look at the code required
to get the app up and running.

We started out with the basic text editor app and substituted it with a *QgsMap-Canvas*. To get that to work, we have to do a bit of setup first.

Figure 12.2: A Simple PyQGIS Application

In *lines 2 and 3* we import the QGIS Python modules. We then have to setup QGIS by setting the prefix path (the location where QGIS is installed) in *line 6* and then initializing it in *line 7* with a call to *QApplication.initQgis*.

Lines 9 through 12 setup the main window and grid layout and are the same as in our simple PyQt app.

In *line 14* we create our *QgsMapCanvas*. When writing a plugin we use the QGIS map canvas; here we have to provide our own.

We want the canvas to fill the application window and do that by adding it to the grid layout in *line 15*.

By default the map canvas has a black background. *Line 16* uses the *setCanvasColor* method to set it to white.

Next we create a *QgsVectorLayer* from a shapefile and add it to the *QgsMapLayerRegistry* in *lines 17-21*. This should look familiar as it is the same method we used in previous chapters.

Even though we have a vector layer, we need to use it to create a canvas layer using *QgsMapCanvasLayer* in *line 22*. We then set the layers on the canvas in *line 23* using the *setLayerSet* method, passing our newly created canvas layer as a list.

To make sure our added layer is visible, we zoom the canvas to the full extent of the shapefile in *line 24*.

The last thing to do is show the main window in *line 26*. Since we want to run the code as a script instead of individually entering statements in the Python shell, we need the *app.exec_()* call in *line 29*, otherwise our application will come up and immediately exit.

That's it—we have a simple, although spartan and inflexible application. Let's refactor it and dress it up a bit in the next section.

12.3   Creating our Own Main Window class

Our code so far is not very modular. To clean things up let's refactor the main window code into it's own class:

Listing 12.3: ourmainwindow_1.py

```
 1  import os
 2
 3  from PyQt4.QtGui import *
 4
 5  from qgis.gui import *
 6  from qgis.core import *
 7
 8
 9  class OurMainWindow(QMainWindow):
10      def __init__(self):
11          QMainWindow.__init__(self)
12
13          self.setupGui()
14
15          self.add_ogr_layer('/data/alaska.shp')
16          self.map_canvas.zoomToFullExtent()
17
18      def setupGui(self):
19          frame = QFrame(self)
20          self.setCentralWidget(frame)
21          self.grid_layout = QGridLayout(frame)
22
23          self.map_canvas = QgsMapCanvas()
```

```
24          self.map_canvas.setCanvasColor(QColor(255, 255, 255))
25          self.grid_layout.addWidget(self.map_canvas)
26
27      def add_ogr_layer(self, path):
28          (name, ext) = os.path.basename(path).split('.')
29          layer = QgsVectorLayer(path, name, 'ogr')
30          QgsMapLayerRegistry.instance().addMapLayer(layer)
31          canvas_layer = QgsMapCanvasLayer(layer)
32          self.map_canvas.setLayerSet([canvas_layer])
```

The *OurMainWindow* class contains much of the code from our original
script, but we've made a start on making it more modular and easier to
understand.

The first thing you should notice is that our class is a subclass of *QMain-
Window* (*line 9*). This allows us to extend *QMainWindow* and add additional
functionality to it.

The *__init__* method sets up our GUI, adds a shapefile, and zooms to full
extent. Ultimately we would want to add methods to our class to choose the
shapefile we want to load.

The *setupGui* method creates the GUI and adds the map canvas to our main
window.

Lastly, the *add_ogr_layer* method takes the path to our shapefile and adds
it to the map, much the way our earlier script did.

You might have noticed something missing. There is no code to actually
create the application and get it running. For that we need another small bit
of code, again abstracted from our original script:

Listing 12.4: our_app_1.py

```
1   from PyQt4.QtGui import *
2   from qgis.core import *
3
4   from ourmainwindow import OurMainWindow
5
6   app = QApplication([])
7   # set up QGIS
8   QgsApplication.setPrefixPath('/dev1/apps/qgis', True)
9   QgsApplication.initQgis()
10
11  # set the main window and show it
```

```
12   mw = OurMainWindow()
13   mw.show()
14
15   app.exec_()
16
17   # "delete" our main window
18   mw = None
19   # clean up QGIS
20   QgsApplication.exitQgis()
```

In `our_app.py` we create the *QApplication* instance, setup the QGIS environment in *lines 8 and 9*, then create an instance of *OurMainWindow* in *line 12*. We then call its *show* method and then start the app in *line 15*. The result looks exactly like our original version shown in Figure 12.2, on page 165.

This app needs a lot more work to make it useful. Let's add some map tools to allow us to control the map view.

12.4   Adding Map Tools to the Application

Since we are using a subclass of *QMainWindow*, our application comes with ready to use areas for menus, toolbars, and status bar. We'll start simple by adding a single map tool to the app—Zoom In.

There is more than one way to add a menu or tool in Qt, however the most flexible way is to use a *QAction*. This allows us to add the action to both the menu and the toolbar, rather than creating code to do both. Here is our action:

```
self.zoomin_action = QAction(
        QIcon(":/ourapp/zoomin_icon"),
        "Zoom In",
        self)
```

This creates the action, but it doesn't do anything yet because it isn't connected to a method to actually zoom the canvas. Here is the new version of `ourmainwindow.py`:

ourmainwindow_2.py

```
1   import os
2
3   from PyQt4.QtGui import *
```

```
4
5    from qgis.gui import *
6    from qgis.core import *
7
8    import resources
9
10
11   class OurMainWindow(QMainWindow):
12       def __init__(self):
13           QMainWindow.__init__(self)
14
15           self.setupGui()
16
17           self.add_ogr_layer('/data/alaska.shp')
18           self.map_canvas.zoomToFullExtent()
19
20       def setupGui(self):
21           frame = QFrame(self)
22           self.setCentralWidget(frame)
23           self.grid_layout = QGridLayout(frame)
24
25           self.map_canvas = QgsMapCanvas()
26           self.map_canvas.setCanvasColor(QColor(255, 255, 255))
27           self.grid_layout.addWidget(self.map_canvas)
28
29           # setup action(s)
30           self.zoomin_action = QAction(
31               QIcon(":/ourapp/zoomin_icon"),
32               "Zoom In",
33               self)
34           # create toolbar
35           self.toolbar = self.addToolBar("Map Tools")
36           self.toolbar.addAction(self.zoomin_action)
37
38           # connect the tool(s)
39           self.zoomin_action.triggered.connect(self.zoom_in)
40
41           # create the map tool(s)
42           self.tool_zoomin = QgsMapToolZoom(self.map_canvas, False)
43
44       def add_ogr_layer(self, path):
45           (name, ext) = os.path.basename(path).split('.')
46           layer = QgsVectorLayer(path, name, 'ogr')
47           QgsMapLayerRegistry.instance().addMapLayer(layer)
48           canvas_layer = QgsMapCanvasLayer(layer)
49           self.map_canvas.setLayerSet([canvas_layer])
50
51       def zoom_in(self):
52           self.map_canvas.setMapTool(self.tool_zoomin)
```

Let's look at the changes needed to get our Zoom In tool visible and work-ing. In *line 8* we import our resources file. This file contains the definition of resources needed in our app, in this case just an icon for the Zoom In tool. The `resources.py` file is created by compiling `resources.qrc` using the `pyrcc4` tool, just as we did in Section 10.4, Modifying the Resources File, on page 139.

The contents of `resources.qrc` are:

```
<RCC>
    <qresource prefix="/ourapp" >
        <file alias="zoomin_icon">resources/mActionZoomIn.png</file>
    </qresource>
</RCC>
```

We also need a graphics file for the toolbar icon—we created a resources subdirectory and copied `mActionZoomIn.png` into it.

We used mActionZoomIn.png found in the QGIS Documentation source: https://github.com/qgis/QGIS-Documentation/tree/master/resources/en/docs/common.

Compiling the resources file gives us `resources.py`:

```
pyrcc4 -o resources.py -o resources.qrc
```

Lines 29 through 42 create the action and setup the zoom in tool. In *line 31* we reference the icon specified in our resource file by using its alias.

We need a toolbar so we create it in *line 35* and name it "Map Tools". Then we can add the action to it in *line 36*. We need to connect the action to a method that will do something when the tool is triggered. In *line 39* we connect it to the *zoom_in* method.

In addition to the action, we need to create the QGIS map tool. This is done in *line 42*, where we create a *QgsMapToolZoom* object, setting its parent to the map canvas and specifying False as the second argument to make it zoom in (setting to True would make a zoom out tool).

The last thing we need is the *zoom_in* method which simply sets the current map canvas tool to our zoom in tool (*lines 51 and 52*).

With that, we can run the app and, as we see in Figure 12.3, on the next page, we now have a toolbar with our zoom in tool and we can use it to manipulate the display. Note the cursor has changed to indicate the zoom in tool is active. You might also have noticed that each time we run the application,

Figure 12.3: A Simple PyQGIS Application with a Zoom In Tool

the fill color of our Alaska shapefile is different. This is because QGIS supplies a random color when a layer is loaded. It will take some additional work to select a color when the layer is loaded.

Here are some enhancements we could add to our simple application:

- Map tools to zoom out, pan, zoom to extent, and zoom full
- Set layer colors
- Select the shapefile to load by providing a file selection dialog box

Obviously we are duplicating existing QGIS functionality with our little app, but it illustrates the concepts in creating a standalone application.

> **Packaging Your Standalone App**
> _____
>
> Packaging your standalone application can be a challenge, but there are some utilities that can help:
> - Linux: Freeze http://wiki.python.org/moin/Freeze
> - Mac: py2app https://pypi.python.org/pypi/py2app/
> - Windows: py2exe http://www.py2exe.org/

12.5   Exercises

1. Add a title to the main window of the app

2. Add some additional map tools to the app: zoom out, pan, and zoom full

3. Add a tool to provide a way to select the shapefile to load

4. Add a button to save the current map to an image file

5. Add the *Select by rectangle* map tool to the application

12.6   Summary

That's it---you've completed your first excursion into the world of PyQGIS programming! For more information, be sure to check out the following resources:

- PyQGIS Cookbook: `http://loc8.cc/ppg/cookbook`
- GIS Stackexchange: `http://gis.stackexchange.com`
- QGIS API documentation: `http://loc8.cc/ppg/api`
- QGIS Documentation: `http://qgis.org/en/docs/index.html`
- QGIS developer mailing list: `http://lists.osgeo.org/mailman/listinfo/qgis-user`

13

Answers to Exercises

13.1   *Exercises: Introduction*

Answers to the exercises in the Introduction chapter:

1. *addProject*

2. *addRasterLayer*

3. *iface.addVectorLayer('/path/to/world_borders.shp', 'world_borders', 'ogr')*

13.2   *Exercises: Python Basics*

Answers to the exercises in the Python Basics chapter:

1. A function to accept x and y values and print to four decimal places:

```
def print_xy(x, y):
    print "X, Y: {:.4f}, {:.4f}".format(x, y)
```

2. Using named parameters

```
print_xy(y=8.2, x=99.991)
```

3. Well Known Text with Z:

```
def wellKnownText(self):
    return u"POINT Z({:.2f}, {:.2f}, {:.2f})".format(self.x(), self.y(), self.z())
```

13.3   Exercises: The QGIS/Python Ecosystem

Answers to the exercises in The QGIS/Python Ecosystem chapter:

1. Install *ScriptRunner* and *Plugin Builder*:

   a. Click on `Plugins->Manage and Install Plugins...` in the menu

   b. Use the *Filter* box to locate each plugin

   c. Click the *Install plugin* button to install each

2. Locate *ScriptRunner* and *Plugin Builder* in the `Plugins` menu:

   - `Plugins->ScriptRunner->ScriptRunner`
   - `Plugins->Plugin Builder...->Plugin Builder`

3. Use the mouse to hover over each icon in the `Plugins` toolbar to locate each plugin

4. Disable *ScriptRunner* using the *Plugin Manager*:

   a. Click `Plugins->Manage Plugins...` in the menu

   b. Find *ScriptRunner* in the list, using the *Filter* box if needed

   c. Uncheck the box to the left of *ScriptRunner*

   d. Click OK

   e. Examine the menu and toolbar for changes

5. At a minimum, you should find the `scriptrunner` and `pluginbuilder` plugins in your plugin directory, along with any other plugins that may have been installed.

13.4   Exercises: Using the Console

Answers to the exercises in the Using the Console chapter:

1. Load the world_borders layer:

```
wb = iface.addVectorLayer('/data/world_borders.shp', 'world_borders', 'ogr')
```

2. Change the color to green with 50% transparency. You need to import QColor in order for this work:

```
from PyQt4.QtGui import QColor
renderer = wb.rendererV2()
symbol = renderer.symbol()
symbol.setColor(QColor(0, 255, 0))
symbol.setAlpha(0.5)
```

3. Update the layer and legend

```
iface.legendInterface().refreshLayerSymbology(wb)
iface.mapCanvas().refresh()
```

13.5 Exercises: Running Scripts

Hints to solving the exercises for the Running Scripts chapter:

1. Use the *QgsVectorLayer.isValid()* method to determine if a layer is valid and respond accordingly

2. The *change_color* method should accept a color value as an argument. Test the color to see if it contains commas, and if so assume it is an RGBA string:

```
if ',' in color:
    (red, green, blue, alpha) = color.split(',')
    new_color = QColor.fromRgb(int(red), int(green), int(blue), int(alpha))
    transparency = color.alpha() / 255.0
else:
    new_color = QColor(color)
    transparency = None
```

Use *symbol.setColor* to set the new color and if transparency is not None, use *symbol.setAlpha* to set the transparency.

3. Modify *load_layer* to accept a path name as an argument. Modify the creation of the *QgsVectorLayer* object to use the path and the basename of the file as its label in the legend (Hint: use *os.path.basename*).

4. Extra credit. Hint: use *iface.addRasterLayer*

13.6   Exercises: Tips and Techniques

1. You'll find `qgis.utils.py` in the same directory as `qgis.core` and `qgis.gui`.

2. Use the URI method found in Section 8.1, Memory Layers, on page 86.

3. Extra credit—you're on your own.

4. Use a *QInputDialog.getText* to get the new name, then get the object (*QgsFeature*) for the selected feature. Modify the name and update the attribute table using the data provider method. See Section 8.6, Editing Attributes, on page 101 for hints.

13.7   Exercises: Extending the API

1. Add error checking for invalid colors. Look for other issues that need handling.

2. Extra credit—you're on your own.

3. Use the information in Section 8.4, Working with Symbology, on page 91 to create the fill and apply it.

4. See Section 8.3, Working with Databases, on page 89 for hints on how to contruct the URI.

5. See Section 8.1, Loading Vector Layers, on page 85.

13.8   Exercises: Writing Plugins

Answers/hints to the exercises in the Writing Plugins chapter:

1. Add format specifiers to

   ```
   coords = "{}, {}".format(point.x(), point.y())
   ```

   in the *display_point* function.

2. Using Qt Designer remove the Line Edit widget and replace it with a Label widget. Modify the code to reference the new widget in the *display_point* function. Be sure to compile your UI changes using

pyuic4.

3. Use the *setSelection* method of *QLabel* to select the text when the new *QToolButton* is clicked, then copy it to the clipboard using QClipboard. You will need to connect the *triggered* signal of the button to a new method that selects the text and copies it to the clipboard. Test your work by pasting into your text editor.

4. Use Qt Designer to apply a grid layout to your dialog. Save the changes, compile the UI using pyuic4, then test the plugin.

5. Extra credit—save the coordinates found in *self.dlg.userPos* using *QSettings*, then restore it in *WhereAmI.__init__*.

13.9   Exercises: Writing a Standalone Application

Answers/hints to the Writing a Standalone Application chapter:

1. Use the *setWindowTitle* method of your main window object to set the title in our_app.py:

   ```
   mw.setWindowTitle('My Fancy Title')
   ```

2. Use the code for *zoom_in* as an example to add additional tools. Don't forget to create a *QAction* for each tool and connect it to a method that calls *self.map_canvas.setMapTool*.

3. Create a *QAction* for loading a shapefile and add it to the toolbar. Connect the tool to a method that uses *QFileDialog.getOpenFileName* to get the path from the user, then call *add_ogr_layer* using the path.

4. Create a *QAction* for saving to an image file and connect it to a method that uses *QgsMapCanvas.saveAsImage* to save it.

5. Use the same methodology as in number 2 to add the tool.

14

Appendix A: Installing QGIS

The installation instructions in this appendix are geared towards getting you a functional install to support programming with PyQGIS.

This section describes how to install QGIS on Linux, OS X, and Windows, as well as providing a resource for building QGIS from source.

14.1   Installing QGIS on Windows with OSGeo4W

Using the OSGeo4W standalone installer will give you a complete working environment for developing with PyQGIS. Follow these steps to install QGIS, GDAL, and other tools you'll need:

1. Download the standalone installer from `http://loc8.cc/ppg/get_qgis`

2. Run the installer

3. All the defaults for the install are fine, with the exception of installation directory. Be sure to choose `C:\qgis_2.0` or another directory name that does **not** contain spaces.

To use the interactive Python interpreter we need to add a couple of environment settings. Create a file named `pyqgis.cmd` and save it in a convenient location. The file should contain:

```
set PATH=%PATH%;C:\qgis_2.0\apps\qgis\bin
set PYTHONPATH=C:\qgis_2.0\apps\qgis\python
```

To use Python from the command line, run the OSGeo4W shell that was installed with QGIS and then execute the `pyqgis.cmd` script. You now have full access to the PyQGIS API from the interactive Python shell.

You might want to put pyqgis.cmd in your path to make it easy to run from any directory.

14.2   Installing QGIS on Mac OS X

The OS X version of QGIS is provided as an installer for Lion/Mountain Lion and Snow Leopard at `http://loc8.cc/ppg/kyngchaos`.

To install QGIS, first download and install the GDAL Complete framework package, available from the same page. Then install the appropriate QGIS package.

In order to access the QGIS libraries from Python (outside of QGIS), you'll need to add the following to your environment:

- QGISBASE=/Applications/QGIS.app/Contents
- export DYLD_LIBRARY_PATH=$QGISBASE/MacOS/lib
- export PYTHONPATH=$QGISBASE/Resources/python

You can do this from a shell script that you source each time you want to use the libraries, or add them permanently to your $HOME/.bash_profile. Be sure to set QGISBASE to the location of you QGIS application (by default /Applications/QGIS.app).

14.3   Installing QGIS on Linux

The downloads page[31] provides instructions for installing QGIS on the following Linux distributions:

- Debian
- Fedora
- RHEL / CentOS / Scientific Linux
- openSUSE

---

[31] http://loc8.cc/ppg/get_qgis

- Mandriva
- Ubuntu
- Slackware

To install, select the appropriate distribution and follow the instructions.

14.4   Building QGIS

If your operating system/version isn't supported, you can build QGIS from source. This is not a trivial effort as there are a number of dependencies and build tools required to compile QGIS. This topic is outside the scope of this book, however, detailed build instructions can be found in the INSTALL document[32] in the QGIS source distribution.

[32] http://loc8.cc/ppg/INSTALL

15

Appendix B: Code Listings

🖉 You can download all the code listed in this book at `http://locatepress.com/ppg/data_code`.

15.1 wrapper.py

Listing 15.1: wrapper.py

```python
1   import os
2
3   from PyQt4.QtGui import *
4
5   from qgis.utils import iface
6   from qgis.core import *
7
8   from osgeo import ogr
9   from osgeo import gdal
10
11
12  def addLayer(uri, name=None):
13      """ Generic attempt to add a layer by attempting to
14          open it in various ways"""
15      # try to open using ogr
16      lyr = ogr.Open(uri)
17      if lyr:
18          return addOgrLayer(uri, name)
19      else:
20          # try to open using gdal
21          lyr = gdal.Open(uri)
22          if lyr:
23              return addGdalLayer(uri, name)
```

```
24          else:
25              return None
26
27
28  def addOgrLayer(layerpath, name=None):
29      """ Add an OGR layer and return a reference to it.
30          If name is not passed, the filename will be used
31          in the legend.
32
33          User should check to see if layer is valid before
34          using it."""
35      if not name:
36          (path, filename) = os.path.split(layerpath)
37          name = filename
38
39      lyr = QgsVectorLayer(layerpath, name, 'ogr')
40      return QgsMapLayerRegistry.instance().addMapLayer(lyr)
41
42
43  def addGdalLayer(layerpath, name=None):
44      """"Add a GDAL layer and return a reference to it"""
45      if not name:
46          (path, filename) = os.path.split(layerpath)
47          name = filename
48
49      lyr = QgsRasterLayer(layerpath, name)
50      return QgsMapLayerRegistry.instance().addMapLayer(lyr)
51
52
53  def removeLayer(layer):
54      QgsMapLayerRegistry.instance().removeMapLayer(layer.id())
55
56
57  def createRGBA(color):
58      (red, green, blue, alpha) = color.split(',')
59      return QColor.fromRgb(int(red), int(green), int(blue), int(alpha))
60
61
62  def changeColor(layer, color):
63      """ Change the color of a layer using
64          Qt named colors, RGBA, or hex notation."""
65      if ',' in color:
66          # assume rgba color
67          color = createRGBA(color)
68      else:
69          color = QColor(color)
70
71      renderer = layer.rendererV2()
72      symb = renderer.symbol()
73      symb.setColor(color)
```

```
74    layer.setCacheImage(None)
75    iface.mapCanvas().refresh()
76    iface.legendInterface().refreshLayerSymbology(layer)
```

15.2 WhereAmI Plugin

Listing 15.2: __init__.py

```
1    # -*- coding: utf-8 -*-
2    """
3    /***************************************************************************
4     WhereAmI
5                                     A QGIS plugin
6     Display coordinates of a map click
7                                 -------------------
8            begin              : 2013-12-07
9            copyright          : (C) 2014 by gsherman
10           email              : gsherman@geoapt.com
11    ***************************************************************************/
12
13    /***************************************************************************
14     *
       *
15     *   This program is free software; you can redistribute it and/or modify
       *
16     *   it under the terms of the GNU General Public License as published by
       *
17     *   the Free Software Foundation; either version 2 of the License, or
       *
18     *   (at your option) any later version.
       *
19     *
       *
20    ***************************************************************************/
21    This script initializes the plugin, making it known to QGIS.
22    """
23
24
25    def classFactory(iface):
26        # load WhereAmI class from file WhereAmI
27        from whereami import WhereAmI
28        return WhereAmI(iface)
```

Listing 15.3: whereami.py

```
1    # -*- coding: utf-8 -*-
2    """
3    /***************************************************************************
4     WhereAmI
5                                     A QGIS plugin
```

```
 6    Display coordinates of a map click
 7                        -------------------
 8        begin                 : 2013-12-07
 9        copyright             : (C) 2014 by gsherman
10        email                 : gsherman@geoapt.com
11    ***********************************************************************/
12
13    /***********************************************************************
14    *                                                                     *
15    *  This program is free software; you can redistribute it and/or modify *
16    *  it under the terms of the GNU General Public License as published by *
17    *  the Free Software Foundation; either version 2 of the License, or   *
18    *  (at your option) any later version.                                 *
19    *                                                                     *
20    ***********************************************************************/
21    """
22    import os
23    # Import the PyQt and QGIS libraries
24    from PyQt4.QtCore import *
25    from PyQt4.QtGui import *
26    from qgis.core import *
27    from qgis.gui import QgsMapToolEmitPoint
28    # Initialize Qt resources from file resources.py
29    import resources_rc
30    # Import the code for the dialog
31    from whereamidialog import WhereAmIDialog
32
33
34    class WhereAmI:
35
36        def __init__(self, iface):
37            # Save reference to the QGIS interface
38            self.iface = iface
39            # Create the dialog and keep reference
40            self.dlg = WhereAmIDialog()
41            # initialize plugin directory
42            self.plugin_dir = os.path.join(
43                QFileInfo(QgsApplication.qgisUserDbFilePath()).path(),
44                "/python/plugins/whereami")
45
46            # Store reference to the map canvas
47            self.canvas = self.iface.mapCanvas()
48            # Create the map tool using the canvas reference
49            self.pointTool = QgsMapToolEmitPoint(self.canvas)
50
51            # initialize locale
52            localePath = ""
53            locale = QSettings().value("locale/userLocale")[0:2]
54
55            if QFileInfo(self.plugin_dir).exists():
```

```
56            localePath = self.plugin_dir + "/i18n/whereami_" + locale + ".qm"
57
58        if QFileInfo(localePath).exists():
59            self.translator = QTranslator()
60            self.translator.load(localePath)
61
62            if qVersion() > '4.3.3':
63                QCoreApplication.installTranslator(self.translator)
64
65    def initGui(self):
66        # Create action that will start plugin configuration
67        self.action = QAction(
68            QIcon(":/plugins/whereami/whereami_icon.png"),
69            u"Where Am I?", self.iface.mainWindow(),
70            toolTip='Show me where I am',
71            triggered=self.run)
72        # connect signal that the canvas was clicked
73        self.pointTool.canvasClicked.connect(self.display_point)
74
75        # Add toolbar button and menu item
76        self.iface.addToolBarIcon(self.action)
77        self.iface.addPluginToMenu(u"&Where Am I?", self.action)
78
79    def unload(self):
80        # Remove the plugin menu item and icon
81        self.iface.removePluginMenu(u"&Where Am I?", self.action)
82        self.iface.removeToolBarIcon(self.action)
83
84    def display_point(self, point, button):
85        # report map coordinates from a canvas click
86        self.dlg.hide()
87        coords = "{}, {}".format(point.x(), point.y())
88        self.dlg.ui.lineEdit.setText(str(coords))
89        # show the dialog
90        if self.dlg.userPos is not None:
91            self.dlg.move(self.dlg.userPos)
92        self.dlg.show()
93
94    # run method that performs all the real work
95    def run(self):
96        # set the map tool
97        self.canvas.setMapTool(self.pointTool)
```

Listing 15.4: whereamidialog.py

```
1  # -*- coding: utf-8 -*-
2  """
3  /***************************************************************************
4   WhereAmIDialog
5                                   A QGIS plugin
```

```
6    Display coordinates of a map click
7                         -------------------
8         begin                : 2013-12-07
9         copyright            : (C) 2014 by gsherman
10        email                : gsherman@geoapt.com
11    ***********************************************************************/
12
13   /***********************************************************************
14    *                                                                   *
15    *  This program is free software; you can redistribute it and/or modify *
16    *  it under the terms of the GNU General Public License as published by *
17    *  the Free Software Foundation; either version 2 of the License, or   *
18    *  (at your option) any later version.                                *
19    *                                                                   *
20    ***********************************************************************/
21    """
22
23   from PyQt4 import QtCore, QtGui
24   from ui_whereami import Ui_WhereAmI
25   # create the dialog for zoom to point
26
27
28   class WhereAmIDialog(QtGui.QDialog):
29       def __init__(self):
30           QtGui.QDialog.__init__(self)
31           # Set up the user interface from Designer.
32           self.ui = Ui_WhereAmI()
33           self.ui.setupUi(self)
34           # attribute for storing the position of the dialog
35           self.userPos = None
36
37       def moveEvent(self, event):
38           self.userPos = event.pos()
```

Listing 15.5: resources.qrc

```
1    <RCC>
2        <qresource prefix="/plugins/whereami" >
3            <file>whereami_icon.png</file>
4        </qresource>
5    </RCC>
```

15.3   Standalone Application

Listing 15.6: our_app.py

```
1    from PyQt4.QtGui import *
2    from qgis.core import *
3
4    from ourmainwindow import OurMainWindow
```

```
5
6   app = QApplication([])
7   # set up QGIS
8   QgsApplication.setPrefixPath('/dev1/apps/qgis', True)
9   QgsApplication.initQgis()
10
11  # set the main window and show it
12  mw = OurMainWindow()
13  mw.show()
14
15  app.exec_()
16
17  # "delete" our main window
18  mw = None
19  # clean up QGIS
20  QgsApplication.exitQgis()
```

Listing 15.7: ourmainwindow.py

```
1   import os
2
3   from PyQt4.QtGui import *
4
5   from qgis.gui import *
6   from qgis.core import *
7
8   import resources
9
10
11  class OurMainWindow(QMainWindow):
12      def __init__(self):
13          QMainWindow.__init__(self)
14
15          self.setupGui()
16
17          self.add_ogr_layer('/data/alaska.shp')
18          self.map_canvas.zoomToFullExtent()
19
20      def setupGui(self):
21          frame = QFrame(self)
22          self.setCentralWidget(frame)
23          self.grid_layout = QGridLayout(frame)
24
25          self.map_canvas = QgsMapCanvas()
26          self.map_canvas.setCanvasColor(QColor(255, 255, 255))
27          self.grid_layout.addWidget(self.map_canvas)
28
29          # setup action(s)
30          self.zoomin_action = QAction(
31              QIcon(":/ourapp/zoomin_icon"),
```

```
32                    "Zoom In",
33                    self)
34            # create toolbar
35            self.toolbar = self.addToolBar("Map Tools")
36            self.toolbar.addAction(self.zoomin_action)
37
38            # connect the tool(s)
39            self.zoomin_action.triggered.connect(self.zoom_in)
40
41            # create the map tool(s)
42            self.tool_zoomin = QgsMapToolZoom(self.map_canvas, False)
43
44        def add_ogr_layer(self, path):
45            (name, ext) = os.path.basename(path).split('.')
46            layer = QgsVectorLayer(path, name, 'ogr')
47            QgsMapLayerRegistry.instance().addMapLayer(layer)
48            canvas_layer = QgsMapCanvasLayer(layer)
49            self.map_canvas.setLayerSet([canvas_layer])
50
51        def zoom_in(self):
52            self.map_canvas.setMapTool(self.tool_zoomin)
```

Listing 15.8: resources.qrc

```
1   <RCC>
2       <qresource prefix="/ourapp" >
3           <file alias="zoomin_icon">resources/mActionZoomIn.png</file>
4       </qresource>
5   </RCC>
```

16

Appendix C: Porting Scripts to 2.0

At QGIS 2.0, a number of classes and methods were removed or changed. Scripts designed to work with QGIS 1.8 are likely to fail under 2.0. The new Plugin Manager detects old or incompatible plugins and won't offer them for installation.

Porting scripts from 1.x to 2.0 can be a matter of trial and error. The QGIS wiki has a list of the changes from 1.8 to 2.0[33], as well as a summary of changes in the API.[34]

16.1 Changes in __init__.py and metadata.txt

At 2.0, metadata.txt contains the information needed to recognize and initialize a plugin in Plugin Manager. Previously the __init__.py script contained all this information. Now it only needs to implement the *classFactory(iface)* function.

Here is a sample metadata.txt file from the WhereAmI plugin:

```
# Mandatory items:

[general]
name=Display coordinates of a map click
qgisMinimumVersion=2.0
description=Display coordinates of a map click
version=0.1
author=gsherman
email=gsherman@geoapt.com
```

[33] http://loc8.cc/ppg/api_changes
[34] http://loc8.cc/ppg/api_changes_2

```
# end of mandatory metadata

# Optional items:

# Uncomment the following line and add your changelog entries:
# changelog=

# tags are comma separated with spaces allowed
tags=

homepage=
tracker=
repository=
icon=whereami_icon.png
# experimental flag
experimental=False

# deprecated flag (applies to the whole plugin, not just a single version
deprecated=False
```

To ensure your plugin can be loaded, the mandatory items must be present. If you specify a *qgisMinimumVersion* less than 2.0, it won't show up in the Plugin Manager.

16.2   SIP API Changes

At QGIS 2.0, the SIP API was upgraded to version 2. Under the hood, SIP[35] manages the mapping between Python the C++ objects that make up QGIS. SIP creates the *bindings* that allow us to use Python with the QGIS libraries.

With the SIP upgrade, some types were removed and substituted with native Python types. The *QVariant* and *QString* classes are no longer part of the QGIS 2.0 API.

These and other changes are detailed in the *Python Plugin API Changes from 1.8 to 2.0* document.[36] It provides examples and of changes required to migrate a plugin from 1.8 to 2.0.

[35] http://loc8.cc/ppg/sip

[36] http://loc8.cc/ppg/api_changes

17

Index

Books from Locate Press

The Geospatial Desktop provides a foundational level of knowledge for understanding GIS and the open source desktop mapping applications that are available for use, for free, today.

Learn about vector and raster data, how to convert data, interacting with spatial databases, creating new map data, geoprocessing, scripting, and more.

Special sections include focused learning on the Quantum GIS and GRASS GIS software platforms as well as an introduction to other packages.

The Geospatial Desktop is written by the founder of the Quantum GIS project, so you can rest assured that you will be led by one of the most knowledgeable authors on the subject.

The Quantum GIS Training Manual Get the jump-start you need to learn this incredibly popular free desktop mapping and GIS toolset.

Comprehensive and structured, your introduction begins with a quick download of example data, making it easy for you to work your way through the concepts and practical exercises, complete with answers and examples.

Ideal for classroom instruction and self-guided learning, included are all the materials needed to run a five day course on Quantum GIS, PostgreSQL and PostGIS. Content is structured for novice, intermediate and advanced users alike. Seasoned Quantum GIS users will also find tips and new techniques to apply to every mapping project. Windows, Mac OS X, or Linux? It's your choice, this book works for all.

Geospatial Power Tools Everyone loves power tools. The GDAL and OGR utilities are the power tools of the GIS world, and best of all, they're free.

The utilities include tools for examining, converting, transforming, building and analysing data. This book is a collection of the GDAL and OGR documentation, but also includes substantial new content designed to help guide you in using the utilities to solve your current data problems.

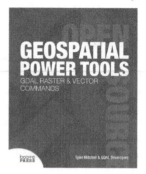

Inside you'll find a quick reference for looking up the right syntax and example usage quickly. The book is divided into three parts:

- Part I - Workflows and examples
- Part II - GDAL raster utilities
- Part III - OGR vector utilities

Once you get a taste of the power the GDAL/OGR suite provides, you'll wonder how you ever got along without them. This book will get you on the fast track to becoming more efficient in your GIS data processing efforts.

Be sure to visit http://locatepress.com for information on new and upcoming titles.

CPSIA information can be obtained at www.ICGtesting.com
Printed in the USA
LVOW02s0520030314

375745LV00005B/11/P